Table of Contents

English Language Arts

Reading: Literature
RL.2.1..4
RL.2.2..6
RL.2.3..8
RL.2.4..10
RL.2.5..12
RL.2.6..16
RL.2.7..18
RL.2.9..20
RL.2.10..22

Reading: Informational Text
RI.2.1...24
RI.2.2...26
RI.2.3...28
RI.2.4...30
RI.2.5...32
RI.2.6...34
RI.2.7...36
RI.2.8...38
RI.2.9...40
RI.2.10...42

Reading: Foundational Skills
RF.2.3..44
RF.2.4..46

Writing
W.2.1..48
W.2.2..50
W.2.3..52
W.2.5..54
W.2.6..56
W.2.7..59
W.2.8..61

Speaking & Listening
SL.2.1...63
SL.2.2...64
SL.2.3...65
SL.2.4...66
SL.2.5...67
SL.2.6...68

Language
L.2.1...69
L.2.2...72
L.2.3...75
L.2.4...78
L.2.5...81
L.2.6...84

Mathematics

Operations & Algebraic Thinking
2.OA.1..88
2.OA.2..90
2.OA.3..92
2.OA.4..94

Numbers & Operations in Base Ten
2.NBT.1..96
2.NBT.2..98
2.NBT.3..102
2.NBT.4..104
2.NBT.5..106
2.NBT.6..112
2.NBT.7..114
2.NBT.8..116
2.NBT.9..118

Measurement & Data
2.MD.1..120
2.MD.2..122
2.MD.3..124
2.MD.4..129
2.MD.5..130
2.MD.6..132
2.MD.7..134
2.MD.8..136
2.MD.9..138
2.MD.10..142

Geometry
2.G.1...146
2.G.2...148
2.G.3...150

©www.CoreCommonStandards.com

Common Core State Standards

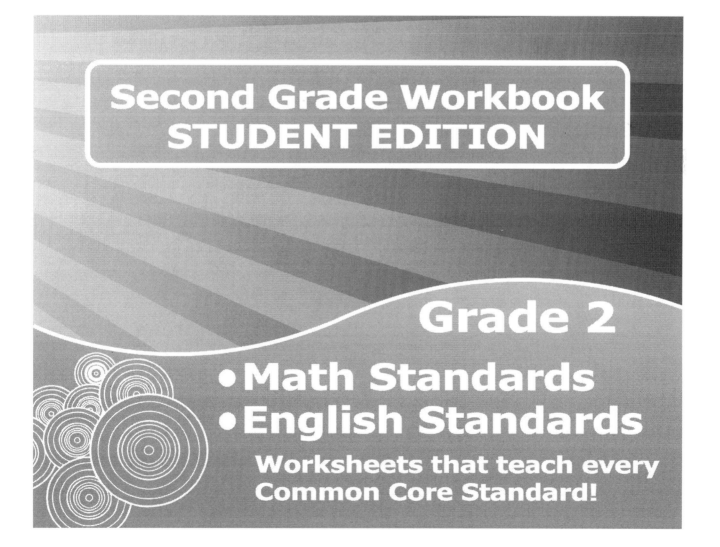

Second Grade Workbook
STUDENT EDITION

Grade 2

- Math Standards
- English Standards

Worksheets that teach every Common Core Standard!

Level: Second Grade Name: _____

Helping

Directions: Read the passage below about helping. Answer the questions about the text. Ask your own questions that can be answered by reading the text.

    I love to help people. Helping people can be lots of fun. I decided to make a list of possible ways that I could help people I know.
    First, I took out my notebook, sat on my bed, and made a list of the people I could help. So far I had thought of my mom, my dad, my little sister Chloe, Mrs. White who lived alone across the street, my next door neighbor Mr. Hill who was always working on his garden, and Mr. and Mrs. Snow who just moved into the yellow house with a puppy.
    Next, I thought about how I could help each person. I know mom always needs help putting laundry away. Dad doesn't like washing his truck. Chloe forgets to put her toys back because she is only 2 years old. Mrs. White has a hard time bringing out her trash on Tuesday nights. Mr. Hill is watering his garden at least 4 times a day because of the hot, sunny weather we have been having. Mr. and Mrs. Snow might need help training their puppy.
    Finally, my list was complete. Now all I had to do was volunteer to help out. I couldn't wait to get started.

Answer these questions about the text.

1. Where does the story take place?

_____

2. How many people are on the child's list?

_____

3. How will he help Mr. Hill?

_____

4. Which job do you think would be the most fun? Why?

_____
_____
_____

Ask two questions about this text.

_____
_____
_____
_____

Standard: Reading l Literature l RL.2.1 ©http://CoreCommonStandards.com

Level: Second Grade   Name: _____

Anticipation

Directions: Read the passage below about anticipation. Answer the questions about the text. Ask your own questions that can be answered by reading the text.

    Finally! The day I had been dreaming about for six months had arrived. Today I was getting my puppy! Mom and dad had decided that it would be a good idea if we waited until school ended to get the puppy. Well school ended yesterday and the big day was here. I woke up early. I made sure I made my bed, brushed my teeth, ate breakfast, and was ready to go by 7 o'clock. Now it was just the wait until the shelter opened.
    We decided that adopting a dog would be the best thing to do. It felt right to give a new home to an unwanted animal. I knew it wasn't going to be an easy decision since there would be a few puppies that I would have to choose from, but I figured the right puppy would somehow let me know that we belonged together.
    It felt like 5 hours had gone by when mom finally said she was ready to go, but when I looked at the clock, it was only 8:45. Hopefully we would be the first ones at the shelter this morning since it would only take us 10 minutes to drive there. I can't wait to see what this summer will bring!

Answer these questions about the text.

1. What is the child anticipating?

_____

2. When does this story take place?

_____

3. What time did the child leave with mom?

_____

4. Where did they go to get the puppy? Why?

_____

_____

Ask two questions about this text.

_____

_____

_____

_____

Standard: Reading I Literature I RL.2.1   ©http://CoreCommonStandards.com

Level: Second Grade   Name: _____

Fables

Directions: Read the Aesop Fable *The Crow and the Pitcher*. Think about what the story is trying to teach.

The Crow and the Pitcher

A Crow, very thirsty, came upon a pitcher which had once been full of water; but when the Crow put its beak into the mouth of the pitcher he found that only very little water was left in it, and that he could not reach far enough down to get at it. He tried, and he tried, but at last had to give up in despair. Then a thought came to him, and he took a pebble and dropped it into the pitcher. Then he took another pebble and dropped it into the pitcher. Then he took another pebble and dropped that into the pitcher. Then he took another pebble and dropped that into the pitcher. Then he took another pebble and dropped that into the pitcher. Then he took another pebble and dropped that into the pitcher. At last, at last, he saw the water mount up near him, and after casting in a few more pebbles he was able to quench his thirst and save his life.

How does the crow feel? How would you feel? What does the crow do? What would you do? What is this story trying to teach us?

_____
_____
_____
_____
_____
_____
_____
_____
_____

Standard: Reading I Literature I RL.2.2   ©http://CoreCommonStandards.com

Level: Second Grade   Name: _____

Fables

Directions: Read the Aesop Fable *The Fox and the Grapes*. Think about what the story is trying to teach.

The Fox and the Grapes

One hot summer's day a Fox was strolling through an orchard when he came to a bunch of grapes just ripening on a vine which had been hung up over a lofty branch. "Just the thing to quench my thirst," said he. Drawing back a few paces, he took a run and a jump, and just missed the bunch. Turning round again with a One, Two, Three, he jumped up, but with no greater success. Again and again he tried after the tempting morsel, but at last had to give it up, and walked away with his nose in the air, saying: "I am sure they are sour."

How does the fox feel? How would you feel? What does the fox say? What would you do? What is this story trying to teach us?

_____
_____
_____
_____
_____
_____
_____
_____

Standard: Reading I Literature I RL.2.2

Level: Second Grade   Name: _____

Rainbow Fish

Directions: Read *Rainbow Fish*. Describe what Rainbow Fish says and does when a little fish asks for one of his scales.

1. Rainbow Fish loves his scales. When a little blue fish asked Rainbow Fish for one of his scales, how did Rainbow Fish react?

   _____

2. Why do you think he reacted that way?

   _____

3. What happened because of the way Rainbow fish reacted?

   _____
   _____

4. What did Rainbow Fish do when no other fish would talk to him?

   _____
   _____

5. How did Rainbow Fish win his friends back?

   _____

6. How did Rainbow Fish feel?

   _____

7. What do you think is the lesson of this story?

   _____
   _____

Standard: Reading | Literature | RL.2.3   ©http://CoreCommonStandards.com

Level: Second Grade   Name: _____

Chrysanthemum

Directions: Read *Chrysanthemum*. Describe what Chrysanthemum says and does when her school friends make fun of her adored name.

1. Chrysanthemum loves her name, bur her friends at school make fun of it. How does she feel after her first day of school?

_____

2. What did Chrysanthemum tell her parents when they asked about her day?

_____

3. How did Chrysanthemum react to how the children treated her?

_____

_____

4. How did Chrysanthemum's parents try to help her? How did Chrysanthemum react?

_____

_____

5. How did Chrysanthemum feel after she met Mrs. Twinkle?

_____

6. What happened that made Chrysanthemum like her name again?

_____

7. What do you think is the lesson of this story?

_____

Standard: Reading l Literature l RL.2.3   ©http://CoreCommonStandards.com

Level: Second Grade   Name: _____

Rhythm and Rhyme

Directions: Read the poem below. Do you hear a rhythm? Do you hear the rhyme?

Crickets make noise in the night.
They rub their wings together tight.
Only males can make the chirp
It doesn't mean that they are hurt.

Crickets chirp so they can mate.
A way they do communicate.
So when you hear songs in the thicket,
You will know it is a cricket.

Answer these questions about the text.

1. Do you hear a rhythm in this poem? How many beats are in each line?

   line 1 _____   line 5 _____
   line 2 _____   line 6 _____
   line 3 _____   line 7 _____
   line 4 _____   line 8 _____

2. What rhymes do you hear?
   _____
   _____
   _____

3. Can you write the next stanza?
   _____
   _____
   _____
   _____

Standard: Reading | Literature | RL.2.4   ©http://CoreCommonStandards.com

Level: Second Grade   Name: _____

Rhythm and Rhyme

Directions: Read the poem below. Do you hear a rhythm? Do you hear the rhyme?

**Obsidian is a rock, you know.
Made from lava cooling fast.
Created from a volcano.
It's black and looks like glass.**

**Obsidian is hard and brittle.
It fractures and becomes quite sharp.
Doctors use it for their scalpels.
Jewelers use it for their art.**

Answer these questions about the text.

1. Do you hear a rhythm in this poem? How many beats are in each line?

line 1 _____   line 5 _____
line 2 _____   line 6 _____
line 3 _____   line 7 _____
line 4 _____   line 8 _____

2. What rhymes do you hear?
_____
_____
_____

3. Can you write the next stanza?
_____
_____
_____
_____

Standard: Reading | Literature | RL.2.4   ©http://CoreCommonStandards.com

Level: Second Grade   Name: _____

Beginnings and Endings

Directions: Choose a story to read. Write how the beginning of the story introduces the characters and main idea of the story. Write how the ending brings everything to a close, solves problems, and answers questions.

The book I chose is:

_____

Written by:

_____

The beginning of the story introduces the characters and how they may interact. It catches the reader's attention. What important things happen at the beginning to introduce the story to the reader?

_____
_____
_____
_____
_____
_____

The end of the story solves the problems that have occurred in the story and resolves events. What happens at the end of the story that brings the story to a close?

_____
_____
_____
_____
_____
_____

Standard: Reading l Literature l RL.2.5   ©http://CoreCommonStandards.com

Level: Second Grade   Name: _____

Beginnings

Directions: Choose two similar stories you have read. Write how the beginning of each story introduces the characters and main idea of the story. Compare how each story's beginnings are similar and different.

Story One	Story Two
_____	_____
Author	Author
_____	_____
Main Character(s)	Main Character(s)
_____	_____
_____	_____

How are Beginnings of these stories similar?

How are the Beginnings of these stories different?

Standard: Reading | Literature | RL.2.5

Level: Second Grade					Name: _____

Endings

Directions: Choose two similar stories you have read. Write how the ending of each story solves problems and resolves events. Compare how each story's endings are similar and different.

Story One	Story Two
_____	_____
Author	Author
_____	_____
Main Character(s)	Main Character(s)
_____	_____
_____	_____

How are the Endings of these stories similar?

How are the Endings of these stories different?

Standard: Reading l Literature l RL.2.5			©http://CoreCommonStandards.com

Level: Second Grade   Name: _____

What Kind of Story?

Directions: With your teacher's help, match the book cover to the type of story it is. (genre)

   poem

   story

                            fantasy

   non-fiction

                            photo-essay

   mythology

                            history

   realistic fiction

                            play

   mystery

                            fable

   fairy tale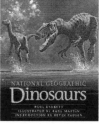

Standard: Reading l Literature l RL.2.5   ©http://CoreCommonStandards.com

Level: Second Grade   Name: _____

Character's Voice and Point-of-View

Directions: Characters in stories have their own points-of-view, or voice. When a character is telling the story, the story is told in a narrative point-of-view. When characters have dialogue in a story, readers use a different voice to represent each character's point of view. Your voice needs to shift so that it echos the style of that character.

In a group, with a partner, or on your own, choose some fictional stories to read. As you read the thoughts or dialogue of the characters, be aware of the character's point-of-view. Use different voices, tones, and rhythms to distinguish between the characters.

Keep track of some of these characters and the type of voice you used.

Character	Type of voice
Snow White	*Slow, sweet, happy, high pitch*

Standard: Reading l Literature l RL.2.6   ©http://CoreCommonStandards.com

Level: Second Grade   Name: _____

Who's Talking Now?

Directions: Using your knowledge of a character's point-of-view, determine which character might be narrating each passage. Who might the narrator be? 3rd-person narrator? 1st-person narrator (a character)?

"But I am not tired!" I tried to tell my mom that I wasn't ready for bed, but from the couch she kept telling me to get into my pajamas. "Let's go Peter," she said. I stormed upstairs and reluctantly put on my Spiderman pajamas. "OK, mom, I am in my pajamas!" No answer. I yelled even louder. "I am in my pajamas!" Back down the stairs I pounded ready to yell it again. I turned the corner into the kitchen and heard, "Surprise!" My whole family was in their pajamas with a bowl of popcorn waiting for me to watch a movie!

Who is telling the story? _____

How do you know? _____

_____

Dad left the CB radio on the table. "Don't touch this Jane. I'll be right back." Jane sat looking at the radio. Her dad had let her talk on it before. She loved the crackling sound it made when someone's voice came through. The little mic snuggled right into the palm of her hand and she reveled in the CB radio jargon... I'm on a flip-flop; freeband; over your shoulder; key up; alligator ahead. A sharp sound snapped Jane out of her daydream. "Breadbox, this is Shark Man...come in." Jane's impulse was to pick up and answer, since Breadbox was her dad's call sign. But her dad said not to touch the radio. The call came in two more times and Jane was just about to answer when her dad walked in and smiled. Standing next to her was his friend, Shark Man. She had passed the no-touch test.

Who is telling the story? _____

How do you know? _____

_____

Everybody left me today! The house was so quiet. I did have a full bowl of kibble and some nice clean water. I decided to just lay on my soft, round bed and play with my squeaky bone. After a good, long nap I heard the doorknob start to turn and that familiar creak of the kitchen door opening. In walked my favorite people. I jumped up and down, my tongue hanging out and my tail wagging like crazy. So glad to be in a family.

Who is telling the story? _____

How do you know? _____

_____

Standard: Reading l Literature l RL.2.6   ©http://CoreCommonStandards.com

Level: Second Grade　　　　　　　　　Name: _____

Text and Illustration Clues

Directions: Look at the illustration below and its caption. Think about the characters and what might be happening in the picture. Answer the questions below with complete sentences.

Beverly and Byron were playing Medieval Soldiers, and once again Byron was winning each battle.

1. How do you think Beverly feels? _____

_____

2. Why do you think she feels this way? How do the picture and text help you? _____

_____

_____

3. Where do you think the children are? Why? _____

_____

4. What do you think might happen next?

_____

_____

_____

5. What makes you think this will happen? _____

_____

Standard: Reading | Literature | RL.2.7　　　　　　　©http://CoreCommonStandards.com

Level: Second Grade   Name: _____

Text and Illustration Clues

Directions: Look at the illustration below and its caption. Think about the characters and what might be happening in the picture. Answer the questions below with complete sentences.

Carl Cochon finished his homework, grabbed a snack, and was allowed a special treat.

1. Where do you think Carl is? Why?_____

_____

2. What do you think Carl is doing? How do the picture and text help you?_____

_____

_____

3. How does Carl feel? Why?_____

_____

4. Who might the other pig be? _____

5. What do you think the other pig is doing? Why?_____

_____

6. What do you think might happen next? _____

_____

Standard: Reading | Literature | RL.2.7   ©http://CoreCommonStandards.com

Level: Second Grade   Name: _____

Comparing Two Stories

Directions: Read two versions of the same story and compare the two stories.

Story One

Main Characters	Setting

Problem	Solution

Story Two

Main Characters	Setting

Problem	Solution

Standard: Reading | Literature | RL.2.9   ©http://CoreCommonStandards.com

Name: _____

Level: Second Grade

The Little Red Hen

Directions: Read the two versions of *The Little Red Hen* and compare the two stories.

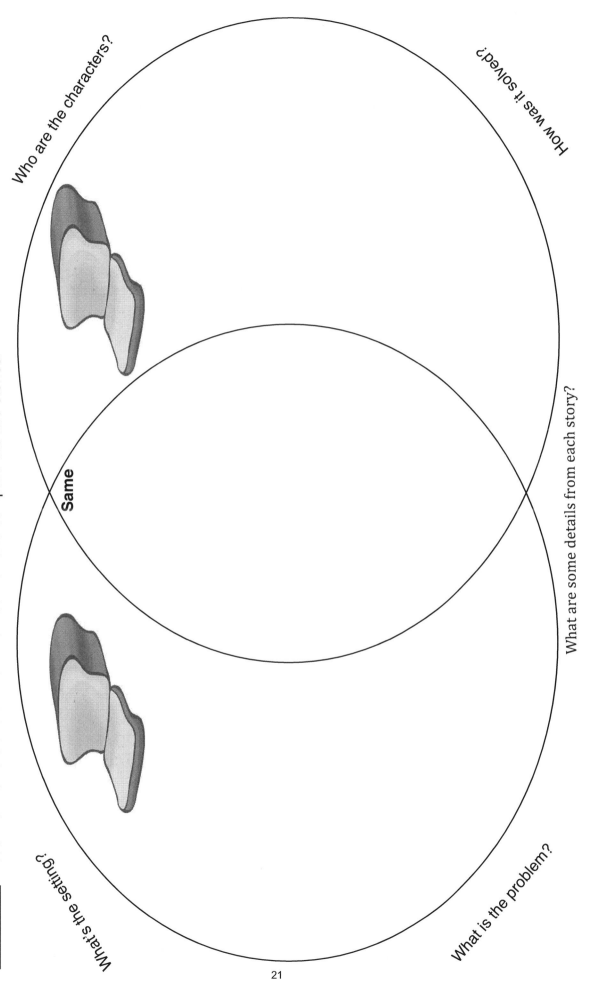

Who are the characters?

How was it solved?

Same

What are some details from each story?

What's the setting?

What is the problem?

Standard: Reading | Literature | RL.2.9

©http://CoreCommonStandards.com

Level: Second Grade   Name: _____

What I Am Reading

Directions: Keep track of the stories you read this year in Second Grade. When you finish a book, write the title and the date you completed the book. Did you like the book?

Date	Book Title	Did You Like the Book?

Standard: Reading l Literature l RL.2.10   ©http://CoreCommonStandards.com

Level: Second Grade   Name: _____

What Are They Reading?

Directions: Keep track of the stories your students can read this year at grade level. Write the date each genre was read successfully.

Date	Book	non-fiction story	realistic fiction story	fantasy story	informational story	poetry

Standard: Reading l Literature l RL.2.10   ©http://CoreCommonStandards.com

Level: Second Grade   Name: _____

Feelings

Directions: Read the passage below about feelings. Answer the questions about the text. Ask your own questions that can be answered by reading the text.

Things that happen to you cause you to have feelings. Sometimes these things make you feel happy, glad, or satisfied, like when you get an A on a test or finish a project. You may feel anxious about meeting new people or worried because you lost your homework. Riding a fast, thrilling roller coaster may make you feel fear, and watching a scary movie may cause terror inside of you.

Sometimes you feel sadness, like when you lose your favorite pet or have a fight with a friend. People often get depressed if they are sad for too long. You can feel anxious about trying something new, or embarrassment if things don't go right. If you have trouble building a toy car or your computer game just won't work, you may feel frustrated. If you just don't understand something, you can feel confused.

Dismay and frustration can quickly turn into anger at times. If you don't feel you were treated fairly, or you can't get what you want, you may feel annoyed, irritated, or outraged. There are times when your feelings get hurt because of what someone has said or done.

Everyone has negative feelings from time to time. Don't be afraid to talk to someone about your feelings. Talking about your feelings can help you solve problems and start feeling better. And, when you feel low, it helps to become optimistic, to think positively, and once again be cheerful. Being kind to others can lift your spirits and help you remain gleeful, energetic, and bright.

Answer these questions about the text.

1. What is this passage about?

   _____

2. When might you feel frustrated?

   _____

3. Why is it important to talk to someone if you are feeling low?

   _____

4. How do you feel when things do not go your way? Explain.

   _____
   _____
   _____

Ask two questions about this text.

_____
_____
_____

Standard: Reading I Informational Text I RI.2.1

Level: Second Grade   Name: _____

Simple Machines

Directions: Read the passage below about simple machines. Answer the questions about the text. Ask your own questions that can be answered by reading the text.

    Rachel is studying about simple machines in her class. Simple machines are tools we use to make work easier. Rachel's homework is to look around her house and find an example of each simple machine. At first, she had a hard time finding even one simple machine. Then Rachel remembered that the things we use everyday may not look like a machine, but they still make work easier.
    So Rachel went into the garage to see what she could find. As she turned the door knob, it occurred to her that this was a *wheel and axle.* One down...five more to go. Rachel walked a few steps and tripped over something. Her dad's hammer! A hammer is a *lever*! Four left. She noticed a basket of laundry next to the washer and looked up to see some drying on a clothesline. The clothesline ended in a *pulley*! This was easier than she had thought.
    Rachel went back inside the house to get a drink. The kitchen door was propped open by a small block slid under the door...a *wedge*! That leaves two simple machines to find. She opened the refrigerator and the handle popped off dropping... a *screw*! Only one left...and she knew just where to find it. Out the front door, to the driveway, she walked up to her brother's skateboard ramp. An *inclined plane*.
    Rachel's homework was complete. She had found all six simple machines. Now she could enjoy her glass of lemonade.

Answer these questions about the text.

1. What is this passage about?

_____

2. Can you name the six simple machines?

_____

3. Where might you find a lever and inclined plane in your home?

_____

4. Why did Rachel have trouble finding simple machines at first?

_____

Ask two questions about this text.

_____

_____

_____

Standard: Reading I Informational Text I RI.2.1

Level: Second Grade   Name: _____

Seeds

Directions: Read the passage below about seeds. What is the main topic of the text? What is the focus of each paragraph? Ask *who, what, where, when, how, why?*

    A seed is a small plant waiting to grow. The seed is covered by a seed coat which protects what's inside. Inside each seed is an embryo. This tiny plant needs water, air, and sunlight to begin to grow, or germinate. Until it gets these things, the seed is dormant.

    The embryo has a temporary food supply, called endosperm, inside the seed. Once the seed coat breaks open, the roots and stem begin to grow. Soon, leaves will grow, which will allow the seed to make it's own food through photosynthesis. Eventually, the plant will grow flowers which will produce new seeds, and the cycle will begin again.

_____
main topic

main focus paragraph 1

main focus paragraph 2

Standard: Reading I Informational Text I RI.2.2

Level: Second Grade   Name: _____

Apollo 11

Directions: Read the passage below about Apollo 11. What is the main topic of the text? What is the focus of each paragraph? Ask *who, what, where, when, how, why?*

    On July 16, 1969, the whole world watched on television as three astronauts were launched into space and sent to the moon for the very first time. The Saturn V rocket launched from Kennedy Space Center in Florida. After dropping the Service Module from the rocket, two of the men entered the Lunar Module which would take them to the moon.

    On July 21, Neil Armstrong became the first man to step onto the surface of the moon. Buzz Aldrin followed him out. The third astronaut, Michael Collins, remained inside the lunar orbit inside the Command Module. As Armstrong stepped onto the moon he said, "That's one small step for man, one giant leap for mankind."

_____
main topic

main focus paragraph 1

main focus paragraph 2

Standard: Reading I Informational Text I RI.2.2

Level: Second Grade   Name: _____

Comparing Events

Directions: After reading an informational story and discussing the events of the story, choose two events, one from each story. Write one way that each event is unique from the other. Then write a piece of information that is common to both.

Story: _____

Author: _____

Event _____   **Event** _____

Something unique about this event.   Something unique about this event.
_____   _____
_____   _____
_____   _____
_____   _____
_____   _____

Something both events have in common.

_____
_____
_____
_____
_____

Standard: Reading I Informational Text I RI.2.3   ©http://CoreCommonStandards.com

Level: Second Grade   Name: _____

How to Make Popcorn

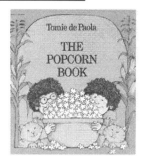

Directions: Read *The Popcorn Book* by Tomie De Paola. Discuss with a partner the steps the boys used to make the popcorn. Work with your partner to write the steps in order to make popcorn. Use time order words like *first, next, then, last* or *first, second, third...*

_____
Title

Standard: Reading l Informational Text l RI.2.3   ©http://CoreCommonStandards.com

Level: Second Grade   Name: _____

Word Meaning

Directions: Read *Earthworms* by Claire Llewellyn. Choose vocabulary from the story to write in the chart below. Use picture information and clues to determine the meanings of these words and phrases.

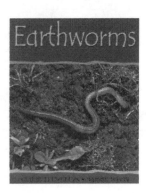

word or phrase

what I think it means

the information I used from the text to help me

word or phrase

what I think it means

the information I used from the text to help me

word or phrase

what I think it means

the information I used from the text to help me

Standard: Reading I Informational Text I RI.2.4   ©http://CoreCommonStandards.com

Level: Second Grade   Name: _____

Rocking Word Meaning

Directions: Read *Let's Go Rock Collecting* by Roma Gans. Choose vocabulary from the story to write in the chart below. Use picture information and clues to determine the meanings of these words and phrases.

word or phrase

what I think it means

the information I used from the text to help me

word or phrase

what I think it means

the information I used from the text to help me

word or phrase

what I think it means

the information I used from the text to help me

Standard: Reading I Informational Text I RI.2.4   ©http://CoreCommonStandards.com

Level: Second Grade   Name: _____

I Can Use Nonfiction Text Features

Directions: Choose different nonfiction books to look at. Find examples of the following nonfiction text features. Write the titles and pages on which you find examples of each. Write a piece of information you learned using the text feature.

Nonfiction Text Feature	Book Title	Page #	Information Learned
drawings			
diagrams			
photographs			
headings			
subheadings			
glossary			
BOLD words			
index			
captions			

Standard: Reading I Literature I RI.2.5   ©http://CoreCommonStandards.com

Level: Second Grade   Name: _____

Using Nonfiction Text Features

Directions: Read *Plants Bite Back* by Richard Platt. Find examples of the following nonfiction text features. Write the pages on which you find examples of each. Write a piece of information you learned using the text feature.

Nonfiction Text Feature	Page #	Information Learned
drawings		
diagrams		
photographs		
headings		
subheadings		
glossary		
BOLD words		
index		
captions		

Standard: Reading I Literature I RI.2.5   ©http://CoreCommonStandards.com

Level: Second Grade   Name: _____

Purpose

Directions: Read the text below about giraffes. Think about what the passage is about and why the author wrote it. Answer the questions.

　　The giraffe is one of the world's tallest mammals. They are known for their long necks, long legs, and spotted body. Giraffes have small horns at the top of their heads that grow to be about 5 inches. These knobs are used to protect from an enemy.
　　Male giraffes are taller than female giraffes and can stand nearly 19 feet tall. Most giraffes can live up to 25 years of age in the wild. They like to roam around in the savannas of Africa. African savannas are mainly dry and are covered with grass.
　　With the giraffe's neck being so long, they are able to eat leaves from tall acacia trees. Giraffes can go many days without drinking water and can live by eating wet leaves.

1. What is this passage about?

   _____

   _____

2. What is the author's purpose for writing this passage?

   _____

   _____

3. What are some details the author writes to support his ideas?

   _____

   _____

   _____

   _____

   _____

Standard: Reading I Informational Text I RI.2.6   ©http://CoreCommonStandards.com

Level: Second Grade   Name: _____

Purpose

Directions: Choose a nonfiction text to read. Think about what the passage is about and why the author wrote it. Answer the questions.

Title:
_____

Type of text: *ex: story, article, essay, informational book...*
_____

Topic:
_____

Why I chose this text:
_____

1. What is this passage about?
_____

2. What is the author's purpose for writing this passage?
_____

3. What are some details the author writes to support his/her ideas?
_____
_____
_____
_____

Standard: Reading I Informational Text I RI.2.6   ©http://CoreCommonStandards.com

Level: Second Grade   Name: _____

Images in Text

Directions: Images in books and magazines help us to better understand the information the author is trying to convey. Look at the images below. How do you think they would contribute to and clarify a text? What could you learn from these images?

image photograph • diagram • drawing	How might it help contribute to (add to) or clarify text (make the text more understandable)?	What could you learn from the image?
What kind of image is this? _____	_____ _____ _____ _____ _____	_____ _____ _____ _____ _____
What kind of image is this? _____	_____ _____ _____ _____ _____	_____ _____ _____ _____ _____
What kind of image is this? _____	_____ _____ _____ _____ _____	_____ _____ _____ _____ _____

Standard: Reading I Informational Text I RI.2.7   ©http://CoreCommonStandards.com

Level: Second Grade   Name: _____

Creating Images in Text

Directions: Images in books and magazines help us to better understand the information the author is trying to convey.
Create an image to help support the text below. You may draw a diagram, sketch a drawing, or even take a photograph.

Ruby-throated Hummingbird Nests

Ruby-throated Hummingbird nests are hard to find. That is because they are so small, just like the Ruby-throated Hummingbird. It is also coated with layers of lichen; a plant made from an alga and fungus that help each other. The nests also are built as high as 60 feet from the ground and may be covered by pine needles, pine cones, or broad leaves. They look more like a bump in the tree than a nest.

When a Ruby-throated Hummingbird begins its nest, the base is made from bud spots and spider webs. The birds collect several webs, eat the spider, and use the silk to build the nest. Then they weave lichen into the nest and attach it to the outside. This creates a hard, outer covering. The inside is made nice and soft when the birds gather thistle, dandelion, or cattail to line it. If you find a Ruby-throated Hummingbird nest that is occupied, you will see the female, for only the females build nests.

Standard: Reading I Informational Text I RI.2.7

Level: Second Grade   Name: _____

Making a Point

Directions: Read an informational piece of text. What is the main point the author is trying to get across? What are the reasons the author gives to support his point? Complete the chart below.

The text I chose is _____

Written by _____

The author is trying to tell us that _____
_____
_____
_____

Here are some reasons the author gives to help support his point that _____
_____
_____

Standard: Reading l Informational Text l RI.2.8

Level: Second Grade   Name: _____

Supporting the Point

Directions: Read the passage below about recycling. What are the reasons the author gives to support recycling?

Recycling is Important

Recycling is an important practice to start early and continue throughout your life. Our beautiful Earth is becoming littered with fast-food wrappers, coffee cups, cigarettes, motor oil, and industrial waste.

Half of the earth's forests are gone and when we throw away paper instead of recycling it to make new paper, we kill more trees. Recycling glass and plastic to make new glass and plastic lessens the amount that goes to the landfill. Some of our trash is incinerated, or burned, which pushes pollutants into the air we breathe. This affects us as humans, the animals we live with, and the plants that grow.

We need to responsibly reuse our waste. Landfills are becoming filled with items that can be reused instead of tossed. Also, poisonous chemicals that leak from discarded products are seeping into the ground, polluting our earth. Trash gets into our waterways and oceans, killing marine life and destroying the only water we have.

We need to repair our broken belongings, or reuse them in new ways. We need to use less and reduce the waste we do create. And we need to teach our children to do the same, so our Earth remains clean enough to support us.

What reasons in the text does the author give to support recycling?

Standard: Reading I Informational Text I RI.2.8   ©http://CoreCommonStandards.com

Level: Second Grade   Name: _____

Comparing Similar Texts: important points

Directions: After reading two different texts about the same topic, complete the chart to compare and contrast the most important point of the text.

What is the *Important Point* the text is trying to make?	_____ _____
Texts	Ways the texts are similar in how the point was presented.	Ways the texts are different in how the point was presented.
Text One Topic _____		
Text Two Topic _____		

Standard: Reading I Informational Text I RI.2.9

©http://CoreCommonStandards.com

Name: _____

Level: Second Grade

Comparing Similar Texts: important points

Directions: After reading two different texts about the same topic, complete the chart to compare and contrast the most important point of the text.

What is the *Important Point* the text is trying to make?		
Texts	Ways the texts are similar in how the point was presented.	Ways the texts are different in how the point was presented.
Text One *Fossils Tell of Long Ago by Aliki* **Topic** *Fossils*		
Text Two *Monster Bones: The Story of the Dinosaur Fossil by Jacqui Bailey* **Topic** *Fossils*		

Standard: Reading | Informational Text | RI.2.9

©http://CoreCommonStandards.com

Level: Second Grade   Name: _____

Nonfiction I Am Reading

Directions: Keep track of the nonfiction text you read this year in Second Grade. When you finish a book, write the title and the date you completed the book. What was the topic?

Date	Book Title	Topic

Standard: Reading I Informational Text I RI.2.10   ©http://CoreCommonStandards.com

Level: Second Grade   Name: _____

What Are They Reading?

Directions: Keep track of the nonfiction text your students can read this year at grade level. Write the date each type of text was read successfully.

Date	Book	non-fiction storybook	photo-graphic essay	auto-biography	informational book	journal/ diary

Standard: Reading I Informational Text I RI.2.10   ©http://CoreCommonStandards.com

Level: Second Grade   Name: _____

Prefixes and Suffixes

Directions: Sometimes root words are changed by adding a part to the beginning of the word (prefix) or to the end of the word (suffix). Read the words below. Underline the prefix or suffix. Write the root word.

Word	Root Word
preheat	
unkind	
breathless	
quickly	
overlook	
defrost	
wonderful	
comfortable	
submarine	
undersea	

Standard: Reading | Foundational Skills | RF.2.3   ©http://CoreCommonStandards.com

Level: Second Grade   Name: _____

Long or Short

Directions: All words have vowels. Read the words below. Listen to the vowel sound in each word. Write whether the vowel is short or long.

word	long or short
fell	_____
quit	_____
stay	_____
luck	_____
tube	_____
feet	_____
kite	_____
flock	_____
strap	_____
steam	_____

Standard: Reading | Foundational Skills | RF.2.3   ©http://CoreCommonStandards.com

Level: Second Grade   Name: _____

Reading With Fluency
nonfiction

Directions: When you read, you are not just saying the words. Readers read with a purpose and to understand. Practice reading orally so that you can be a fluent reader.

Read the passage below while your teacher times you. Try to read as many words accurately as you can in one minute. Try again in a couple of weeks to see if your fluency improves. {Goal of 100 WPM}

The Giant Giraffe

   The giraffe is one of the world's tallest mammals. They are known for their long necks, long legs, and spotted body. Giraffes have small horns at the top of their heads that grow to be about 5 inches. These knobs are used to protect from an enemy.
   Male giraffes are taller than female giraffes and can stand nearly 19 feet tall. Most giraffes can live up to 25 years of age in the wild. They like to roam around in the savannas of Africa. African savannas are mainly dry and are covered with grass.
   With the giraffe's neck being so long, they are able to eat leaves from tall acacia trees. Giraffes can go many days without drinking water and can live by eating wet leaves. How many days do you think you can live without drinking any water?

Date	Words Read Correctly Per Minute

Standard: Reading I Foundational Skills I RF.2.4   ©http://CoreCommonStandards.com

Level: Second Grade   Name: _____

Reading With Fluency
fiction

Directions: When you read, you are not just saying the words. Readers read with a purpose and to understand. Practice reading orally so that you can be a fluent reader.
Read the passage below while your teacher times you. Try to read as many words accurately as you can in one minute. Try again in a couple of weeks to see if your fluency improves. {Goal of 100 WPM}

The Rescued Cat

On a hot, sunny summer day, my dog, Pete, wanted to play,

We went outside happy as can be, until he spotted a cat up a tree!

He barked and barked, but not too loud, this really made me very proud,

Pete wanted to free the frightened cat, but I wasn't sure I was ready for that.

How would I do it? I wondered aloud, the tree was so tall almost touching a cloud,

I couldn't climb, I might fall, unless I find a ladder that was very tall!

A man walked by and saw us stare, he decided to come and help this pair,

He did get a ladder that could reach the cat, and brought him down, just like that!

Pete was happy, and so was I, that this kind man came walking by,

So now everyone is joyful as can be, because that cat is no longer stuck in that tree!

Date	Words Read Correctly Per Minute

Standard: Reading I Foundational Skills I RF.2.4   ©http://CoreCommonStandards.com

Level: Second Grade   Name: _____

Supporting an Opinion

Directions: After reading or listening to various folktales from around the world, write why you think these stories had been handed down from one group of people to another. Use reasons to support your response.

The Argument: _____

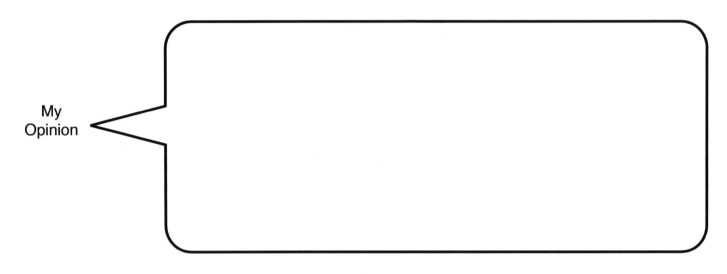

My Conclusion: _____

_____

_____

_____

Standard: Reading I Writing I W.2.1

Level: Second Grade   Name: _____

Opinions and Reasons

Directions: After reading or listening to various folktales from around the world, write why you think these stories had been handed down from one group of people to another. Use reasons to support your response.

_____

Standard: Reading | Writing | W.2.1

Level: Second Grade　　　　　　　　　Name: _____

Inform and Explain

Directions: Write about a topic you choose. Use descriptive words to explain the topic. Provide details, facts, and/or figures to support your writing. Tie your thoughts together with a concluding statement.

　　　The Topic: _____

definitions/
opinions/
explanatory text

supportive details/
facts/figures

My concluding statement: _____

_____

_____

_____

Standard: Reading I Writing I W.2.2　　　　　　　　©http://CoreCommonStandards.com

Level: Second Grade   Name: _____

Inform and Explain

Directions: Write about a topic you choose. Use descriptive words to explain the topic. Provide details, facts, and/or figures to support your writing. Tie your thoughts together with a concluding statement.

_____

Standard: Reading I Writing I W.2.2   ©http://CoreCommonStandards.com

Level: Second Grade   Name: _____

Real Life Narrative

Directions: After reading or listening to a biography of a famous person, write a narrative about the person. Include a main idea based on the character, and a sequence of events from his or her life. Include a strong closing statement. Use the organizer below to prepare your narrative.

Biography Title

_____

Author

_____

Biography Subject

_____

Main Idea

_____

_____

Event	Event	Event
_____ _____ _____	_____ _____ _____	_____ _____ _____

Event	Event	Event
_____ _____ _____	_____ _____ _____	_____ _____ _____

Closing Statement

_____

_____

Standard: Reading | Writing | W.2.3

Level: Second Grade   Name: _____

Fictional Narrative

Directions: After reading or listening to a story with fictional characters, events, and setting, write a narrative about a character from the story. Include a main idea based on the character, and a sequence of events from the story. Include a strong closing statement. Use the organizer below to prepare your narrative.

Book Title

_____

Author

_____

Book Subject

_____

Main Idea

_____

_____

Event	Event	Event
_____	_____	_____
_____	_____	_____
_____	_____	_____

Event	Event	Event
_____	_____	_____
_____	_____	_____
_____	_____	_____

Closing Statement

_____

_____

Standard: Reading I Writing I W.2.3

Level: Second Grade   Name: _____

Work In Progress

Directions: Write about a scientific topic or historical event. Share your writing with a peer. Listen to questions and suggestions your peer has and work together to make your writing better. Edit your writing to correct spelling, punctuation, and grammar. Revise the writing with good word choice.

Level: Second Grade　　　　　　　　　　Name: _____

Work In Progress

Directions: Write a short story about the picture below. Share your writing with a friend. Listen to questions and suggestions your friend has and work together to make your writing better. Edit your writing to correct spelling, punctuation, and grammar. Revise your writing with good word choice.

Standard: Reading | Writing | W.2.5　　　　　　©http://CoreCommonStandards.com

Level: Second Grade   Name: _____

Creating a Powerpoint Presentation

Directions: After reading an informational text about a topic of interest, create a powerpoint presentation to share what you have learned. Use the organizer below to help you plan your powerpoint.

Topic:

slide 1	slide 2
slide 3	slide 4
slide 5	slide 6

Standard: Reading | Writing | W.2.6   ©http://CoreCommonStandards.com

Level: Second Grade   Name: _____

slide 7	slide 8
slide 9	slide 10
slide 11	slide 12

Be sure to edit and revise. Use interesting words, fonts, and colors. Add images and diagrams to help share your ideas.

Standard: Reading | Writing | W.2.6   ©http://CoreCommonStandards.com

Level: Second Grade   Name: _____

Using Digital Resources

Directions: Today, many people use digital tools to write. Use this checklist to record what digital skills each student can perform.

Digital Skill	Date	Success
Uses a mouse well. (Can double-click; move cursor to desired place; scroll if available.)		
Knows where most common characters are on keyboard.		
Knows how to use space bar; back space; delete; and return.		
Can log in and out of programs.		
Can change the font or size of font.		
Can add a graphic.		
Can drag and drop an item.		
Can copy/paste an item.		
Can save a file.		
Can print work.		
Can create a Powerpoint Presentation.		
Can locate information in the internet.		
Can send an email.		
Can attach a file to an email.		

Standard: Reading | Writing | W.2.6   ©http://CoreCommonStandards.com

Level: Second Grade   Name: _____

Research Together

Directions: Work in a group format to research a particular topic. Use various resources to collect information on your topic. Collaborate and work smoothly by assigning roles within your group.

Our Topic: _____

Resources we used: _____
_____
_____

Group members: _____   _____
              _____   _____

My Role: **recorder**   **leader**   **time keeper**   **reader**   **fact checker**

Some information I learned working with my group:
_____
_____
_____
_____

How did I help my group?
_____
_____
_____

Standard: Reading | Writing | W.2.7   ©http://CoreCommonStandards.com

Level: Second Grade   Name: _____

Scientific Observation

Directions: Work in a group format to record scientific observations. Collect data, draw and label diagrams. Make a hypothesis about your observations.

What we are observing: _____

Materials we used: _____

_____

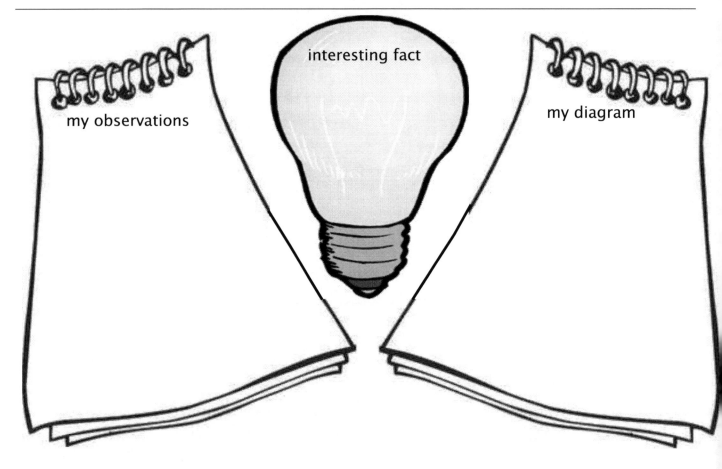

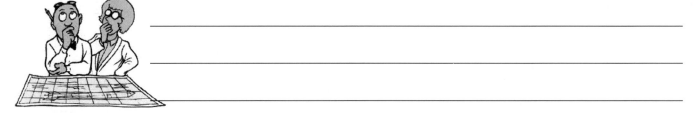

Our hypothesis: _____

_____

Standard: Reading | Writing | W.2.7

Level: Second Grade   Name: _____

Answering a Question

Directions: Read *Bats; Creatures of the Night* by Joyce Milton (or other nonfiction books about bats.) Answer the question below by reading the stories and locating information.

> How is a bat different from all other mammals?

This is some information I found to help me answer the question.

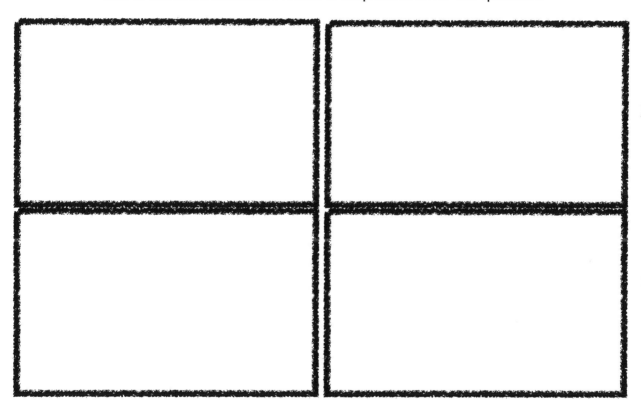

Here is my answer to the question and why I think I am right.

_____
_____
_____
_____
_____
_____
_____

Standard: Reading | Writing | W.2.8   ©http://CoreCommonStandards.com

Level: Second Grade　　　　　　　　　　Name: _____

Answering a Question

Directions: You have a question to answer. Think about the question. Use resources your teacher provides to find information to help you answer the question. Write your answer below.

Here is the question:

I am using resources my teacher gave me.
This is some information I found to help me answer the question.

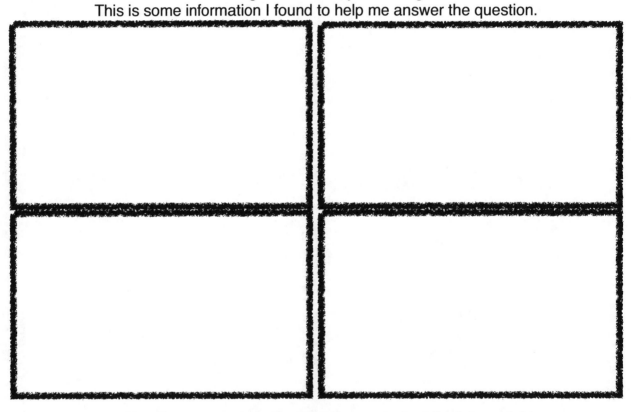

Here is my answer to the question and why I think I am right.

_____
_____
_____
_____
_____
_____
_____
_____

Standard: Reading | Writing | W.2.8　　　　　　　©http://CoreCommonStandards.com

Level: Second Grade   Name: _____

Small Group Discussions

Directions: When we meet for discussions in Second Grade, we contribute to the group by following agreed-upon rules. Use this form during discussions to keep track of how well you participate.

☐ I Wait my Turn and Gain the Floor in a Respectful Way

☐ I Listen To Others

☐ I Stay on Topic

☐ I Respect Others' Ideas

☐ I Ask Questions

☐ I Offer Ideas and Suggestions

Something I learned during today's discussion about _____

was _____

_____

_____

Standard: Reading I Speaking & Listening I SL.2.1   ©http://CoreCommonStandards.com

Level: Second Grade   Name: _____

Taking Notes

Directions: Watch a video about a topic you are studying in class. Think about the information presented and write some key ideas that you heard in the video. Then, share your paper with the class.

Key Idea

Key Idea

Key Idea

Key Idea

Key Idea

*Main Idea

Standard: Reading l Speaking & Listening l SL.2.2   ©http://CoreCommonStandards.com

Level: Second GradeName: _____

Asking Questions to Understand

Directions: Read a true story that is set in another country and perhaps another time. In order to understand more about the culture and the lives of those in the story, ask questions and locate the answers by reading other resources, watching an informative video, or by talking with an expert in that topic. Record the answers in your own words.

Question:

_____

_____

Answer:

_____

_____

_____

Question:

_____

_____

Answer:

_____

_____

_____

Here is what I learned from reading the story and asking my questions:

_____

_____

_____

_____

Standard: Reading I Speaking & Listening I SL.2.3©http://CoreCommonStandards.com

Level: Second Grade   Name: _____

Oral Storytelling

Directions: Listen to a classic story such as *The Pied Piper of Hamelin*, or other fairy tales or fables. As you listen, record important ideas in the organizer below. Orally retell the story using clear, concise language and voice.

Story: _____

Author: _____

Standard: Reading I Speaking & Listening I SL.2.4   ©http://CoreCommonStandards.com

Level: Second Grade					Name: _____

Make an Audio Recording

Directions: Create an audio recording of a poem or story. It can be a story from your classroom collection, the library, or one you or a classmate has written. Use a tape recorder or computer to record your voice. Speak clearly and with interest in order to express the characters' feelings and the events that occur. Don't forget to include your own point of view.

There are several programs available for children to use to create digital stories. Some are listed below.

For Microsoft Products
Photostory ...free program using still photos or graphics and added audio

Powerpoint

For Apple Products
My Story-Book Maker ...App for iPad/iPod/iPhone ($)
    make drawings and record your voice

Writer's Studio ...App for iPad/iPod/iPhone ($)
    make drawings, add photos, and record your voice

iMovie ...usually included in Mac purchase

Keynote (like Powerpoint) included in iWorks

My Story Idea:

_____

_____

_____

Components I will add...

____ computer graphics			____ songs			____ different font

____ scanned photographs		____ speeches			____ bold, italic, underline

____ scanned drawings			____ audio text			____ movie/TV clips

____ computer drawings			____ sound effects		____ video

Standard: Reading | Speaking & Listening | SL.2.5			©http://CoreCommonStandards.com

Level: Second Grade   Name: _____

Speaking in Complete Sentences

Directions: Construct a bridge, tower, or other architectural structure with your choice of materials. Explain to your partner, then the class, using complete, descriptive sentences, how you built the structure. Be sure to add detail and speak in proper sequence.

Write a sentence for each step. Be sure the sentences are complete and use descriptive words.

Step 1
_____
_____
_____
_____

Step 2
_____
_____
_____
_____

Step 3
_____
_____
_____
_____

Step 4
_____
_____
_____
_____

Step 5
_____
_____
_____
_____

Standard: Reading I Speaking & Listening I SL.2.6   ©http://CoreCommonStandards.com

Level: Second Grade   Name: _____

Irregular Plural Nouns

Directions: Most nouns become plural (more than one) by adding -s, or -es to the end of the word. Some nouns, however, don't follow the laws, and the spelling changes to make the noun plural. Read the nouns below. Write their plural forms into the jails.

singular noun	irregular plural form
child	
foot	
mouse	
cactus	
vertebra	
bacterium	
deer	

Standard: Reading | Language | L.2.1   ©http://CoreCommonStandards.com

Level: Second Grade   Name: _____

Irregular Verbs

Directions: Most verbs are made into the past tense form by adding -ed, or just -d. Some verbs, however, don't follow the laws, and the spelling changes to make the verb past tense.
Read the verbs below. Write their past tense forms into the jails.

verb	irregular past tense
sit	
run	
break	
find	
hurt	
weave	
strike	

Standard: Reading l Language l L.2.1   ©http://CoreCommonStandards.com

Level: Second Grade   Name: _____

Collective Nouns

Directions: What's the group name? There are so many different names for different types of groups in the English language. You wouldn't say, "a herd of paper," or "a flock of cows." Choose the best group name for each example.

school   litter   lodge   flock   rookery
bed   herd   pack   colony   swarm

a _____ of beavers
a _____ of ants
a _____ of geese
a _____ of bees
a _____ of buffalo
a _____ of penguins
a _____ of fish
a _____ of snakes
a _____ of puppies
a _____ of wolves

Standard: Reading I Language I L.2.1   ©http://CoreCommonStandards.com

Level: Second Grade   Name: _____

Fixing Sentences

Directions: Read the sentences below. Correct the words that need capital letters, insert proper apostrophes {'}, and add the correct punctuation at the end. { . ! ? }

1	the grasshoppers ears are on its front legs
2	william kirby is known as the father of entomology
3	the bug museum in new jersey is called, *insectropolis*
4	bugz-be-gone pest control came to spray for ants
5	my monarch butterfly collection is bigger than his
6	why does ted the beekeeper wear that net on his head
7	i saw an apple computer at the mall yesterday
8	mrs ferraras class counted 97 mealworms on friday
9	we buy honey to pour in our quaker oatmeal
10	the chicago bulls are my favorite basketball team
11	we all ate chocolate covered grasshoppers at toms party
12	bees are found on every continent except antarctica

Standard: Reading | Language | L.2.2   ©http://CoreCommonStandards.com

Level: Second Grade   Name: _____

Spelling Words

Directions: Look at the rimes below. Place an onset consonant at the beginning of each rime to make new words. You can use single letters or blends. Read the words to a friend.

age	adge	edge
odge	idge	udge

Standard: Reading | Language | L.2.2

Level: Second Grade   Name: _____

Comma Comma

Directions: Commas are used in greetings and closings of letters. They are also used in dates. Write commas where they belong in the letters below.

April 13 1955

Dear Aunt Florence

Mother just told me the good news, that I will be joining you at the farm for summer vacation! I have already begun packing my things and am eager to jump on the train and head north to see you and Uncle Elias.

Until then...
    lovingly
       your niece
          Patricia

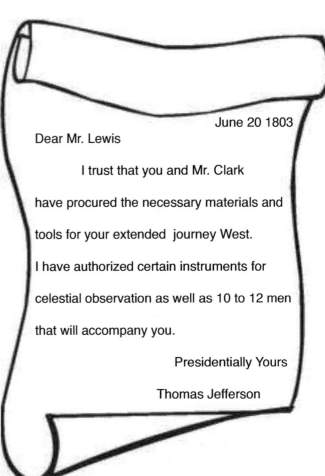

June 20 1803

Dear Mr. Lewis

I trust that you and Mr. Clark have procured the necessary materials and tools for your extended journey West. I have authorized certain instruments for celestial observation as well as 10 to 12 men that will accompany you.

        Presidentially Yours
        Thomas Jefferson

Dear Patrick Susie and Floyd

    Mom and dad have been truly enjoying our vacation in Cape Cod! The sun has been shining and the water has been cool. We miss you all. Hope you are behaving for Nana. See you soon.

Love   Mom and Dad

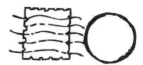

The Garry Family
234 West Willow Ave.
Sioux Falls SD
57006

Standard: Reading I Language I L.2.2   ©http://CoreCommonStandards.com

Level: Second Grade Name: _____

Formal vs Informal

Directions: When we speak to one another, our friends, family, people we meet, we usually use informal language. It is relaxed and doesn't have strict rules.

But there are times that we need to use more formal language: speaking to an employer, polite conversation with strangers, and in certain important types of writing.

Read the sentences below.
Write an **I** if the words are *informal*. Write an **F** if the words are *formal*.

Then, draw a line to match the informal and formal versions of the same sentence.

☐	That stinks.	☐	He may not be correct about that.
☐	It was, like, five bucks, so I was OK.	☐	He found out that the sheep got away.
☐	I think he was totally wrong.	☐	She appears to be upset about something.
☐	His bag contains many things.	☐	That's too bad.
☐	He discovered that the sheep had escaped.	☐	She asked if it was OK.
☐	She asked if it was adequate.	☐	Those kids are wicked noisy.
☐	She seems to be pretty sad.	☐	Whassup with you?
☐	Hello. How are you doing today?	☐	He has a lot of stuff in his bag.
☐	The children there are quite loud.	☐	The item was five dollars and I found that acceptable.

Standard: Reading | Language | L.2.3   ©http://CoreCommonStandards.com

Level: Second Grade   Name: _____

Formal vs Informal

Directions: When do we use informal language? When do we use formal language? Look at the activities below. Think about the setting and who is involved. Write if the activity would use formal or informal language.

write a shopping list _____	phone a friend _____	write a book report _____
explain a procedure _____	phone call to the bank _____	email a family member _____
write a letter to a business _____	give instructions _____	write a text message _____
share a joke with a friend _____	meet your friend's parents _____	make a speech _____
leave a phone message at the doctor's _____	apply for a job _____	write in your journal _____

Standard: Reading l Language l L.2.3   ©http://CoreCommonStandards.com

Level: Second Grade

Name: _____

Formal vs Informal

Directions: Sometimes we need to use formal language when writing. Sometimes we can use informal language when writing. Write a letter to each of the people mentioned below. Think about if the letter should be written informally or formally.

Write a letter to your friend about a new toy you received as a birthday present.

Write a letter to a company about a toy you bought that doesn't work properly.

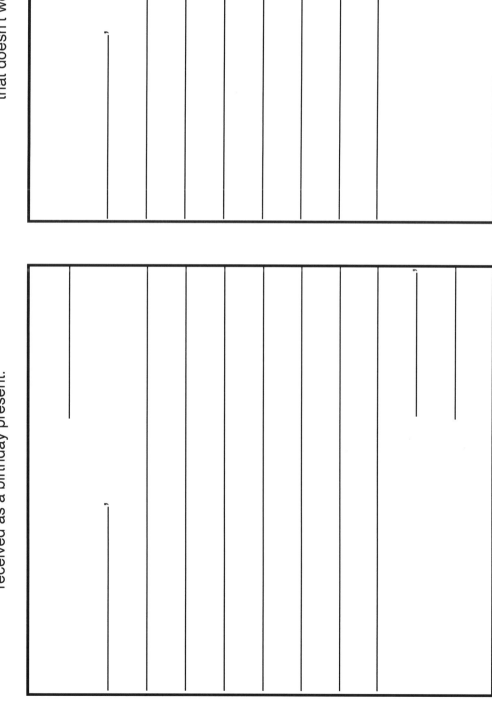

Standard: Reading I Language I L.2.3

©http://CoreCommonStandards.com

Level: Second Grade   Name: _____

Multiple Meanings

Directions: Read the sentences below. Choose a multiple meaning word to complete the partner sentences. Notice how the word is used differently in each sentence.

> ruler   trip   pet   pack   watch
> can   break   cut   fire   sheet   bat

1. I looked at my _____ for the time.   _____ out for that tree!

2. I have a beagle as a _____.   Be gentle when you _____ the pup.

3. _____ I please go to the movie?   The green beans were stored in a _____.

4. Brendan has a _____ on his finger.   Use the scissors to _____ the paper.

5. We went on a _____ last summer.   Don't _____ over that rock!

6. If you're late, he will _____ you.   Let's build a _____ to keep warm.

7. The wolf _____ is howling.   I need to _____ for the trip.

8. A _____ was flying outside at night.   He hit the baseball with a _____.

9. I put a new _____ on my bed.   I wrote a story on a _____ of paper.

10. The chef took a _____.   Please do not _____ the glass.

11. We use a _____ to measure the table.   They elected a _____ for their country.

Standard: Reading I Language I L.2.4   ©http://CoreCommonStandards.com

Level: Second Grade   Name: _____

Multiple Meanings

Directions: Read the words below. Choose 4 multiple meaning words from the list below. Write two sentences for each word showing the different meanings each word can have.

bend	spring	might	stamp	trick	crack	taste
burn	tire	shine	trap	shop	cover	staple

1.

2.

3.

4.

5.

6.

7.

8.

Standard: Reading I Language I L.2.4

Level: Second Grade   Name: _____

Compound Words

Directions: Break the compound word into its two parts. Then write the meaning of the compound word using the parts to describe the whole.

BREAK THE COMPOUND WORD APART   **WRITE A DEFINITION**

birdhouse = ___bird___ + ___house___   *A birdhouse is a house that a bird lives in.*

1. lighthouse = _____ + _____   _____

2. housefly   = _____ + _____   _____

3. bookshelf = _____ + _____   _____

4. notebook   = _____ + _____   _____

5. bookmark   = _____ + _____   _____

6. bedroom   = _____ + _____   _____

7. cookbook   = _____ + _____   _____

8. classroom = _____ + _____   _____

9. lunchroom = _____ + _____   _____

10. clipboard = _____ + _____   _____

Directions: Choose one compound word from above. Draw a picture for each word separately, then draw a picture of the compound word.

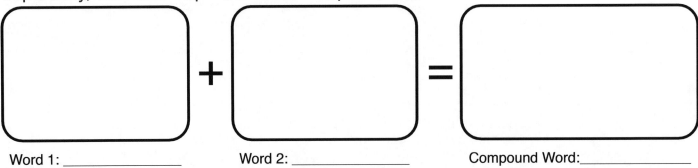

Word 1: _____   Word 2: _____   Compound Word: _____

Standard: Reading | Language | L.2.4   ©http://CoreCommonStandards.com

Level: Second Grade   Name: _____

Figurative Language

Directions: When speaking or writing, use various vocabulary words to give detail or express emotion. Read the lists of words below. Write them in order of intensity from least to greatest.

1. cold   freezing   cool   warm

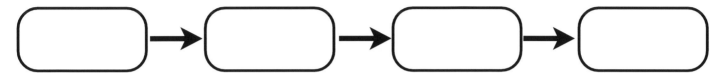

2. content   happy   excited   dissatisfied

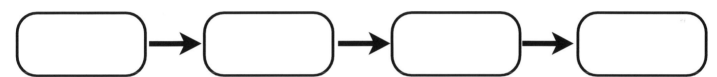

3. large   tiny   average   huge

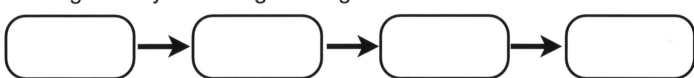

4. whisper   talk   shout   yell

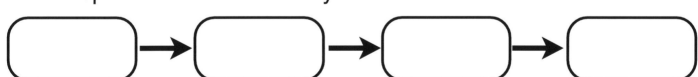

5. frustrated   angry   mad   furious

Standard: Reading I Language I L.2.5

Level: Second Grade   Name: _____

Word Relationships

Directions: It's your turn on the game show! Come up with things that fit each category before the time runs out! Write things that are juicy, sharp, spicy, and hot in the "pyramid" below.

Things that are juicy.

Things that are sharp.

Things that are spicy.

Things that are hot.

Standard: Reading | Language | L.2.5   ©http://CoreCommonStandards.com

Level: Second Grade   Name: _____

Figurative Language

Directions: Words can have similar meanings, but some words are better to use than others. Choose the best word for each sentence.

I will _____ the ball to the baby.

I will _____ the ball at the target.

I will _____ the ball to the batter.

toss
throw
hurl

Mom will _____ around the track.

Mom will _____ to catch the ball.

Mom will _____ the dog at night.

run
walk
jog

My sister _____ when she sees her favorite singer.

My sister _____ when I touch her diary.

My sister _____ on the phone all night!

talks
screams
yells

Paul _____ at the paintings in the museum.

Paul _____ at me as I steal his brownie.

Paul _____ out the window at the stars.

stares
looks
glares

Standard: Reading I Language I L.2.5   ©http://CoreCommonStandards.com

Level: Second Grade   Name: _____

Describing

Directions: Read *Sarah, Plain and Tall by* Patricia MacLachlan. Talk about Sarah and Caleb with a partner.

After reading chapter one...

Describe what you know about Caleb and Anna.
What kind of characters are they? How would you describe them?

_____

_____

_____

_____

_____

After reading chapter six...

What do you think it meant when the words said, "And Sarah was happy." Explain why Sarah was happy at this point.

_____

_____

_____

_____

After reading chapter eight...

Think about a time you were in the middle of a big storm. Describe how you felt, what you did, and what you saw.

_____

_____

_____

_____

Standard: Reading | Language | L.2.6   ©http://CoreCommonStandards.com

Level: Second Grade   Name: _____

Describing

Directions: Read *Who Has Seen the Wind?* by Christina Rossetti. Talk about the poem with a partner.

Visualize being in the poem.
What do you feel? What do you smell? What do you see?

Describe the world inside the poem.
Use descriptive adjectives (describe nouns) and adverbs (describe verbs).

_____

_____

_____

_____

_____

_____

_____

_____

Why do you think Christina Rossetti wrote this poem?

_____

_____

_____

Standard: Reading I Language I L.2.6

Level: Second Grade   Name: _____

Describing

Directions: Read *Arthur's Computer Disaster* by Marc Brown. Talk about the story with a partner.

Think about how Arthur felt when he used his mom's computer without permission and accidentally broke it.

Describe a time that you did something wrong and how you felt about it afterwards. Use words that describe your feelings, emotional (mind) and physical (body).

_____

_____

_____

_____

_____

_____

_____

_____

How did you feel at the end of the story?

_____

_____

_____

Standard: Reading | Language | L.2.6

Common Core State Standards

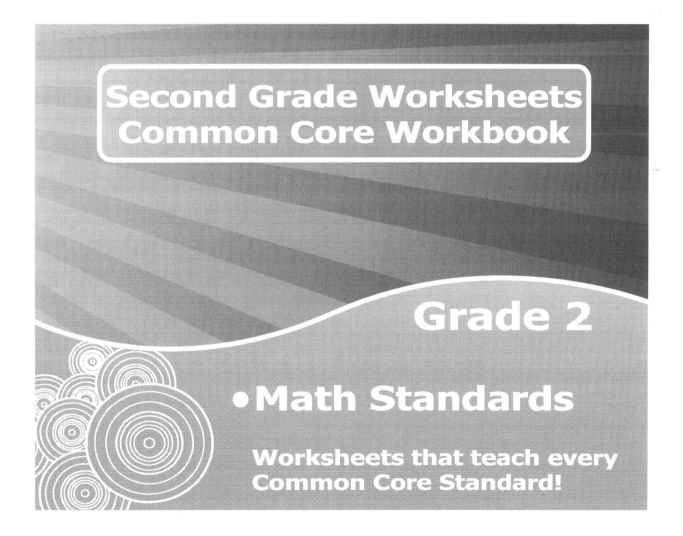

Second Grade Worksheets
Common Core Workbook

Grade 2

Math Standards

Worksheets that teach every Common Core Standard!

Level: Second Grade   Name: _____

Adding and Subtracting Number Stories

Directions: Read the number stories below. Think about what information is important. Think about whether you should add or subtract. Draw pictures and equations to help you work out the problems.

Julie had 13 Hershey Kisses. Stacy had 9 Hershey Kisses. Steve gave Julie 9 more Hershey Kisses. How many Hershey Kisses does Julie have now?

_____ Hershey Kisses

Lionel brought 55 cupcakes to school. There were chocolate, vanilla, and strawberry flavors. Jarod took 5 of the cupcakes to the office. Laura took 8 of them to the teacher's lounge. Nick ate 2. How many cupcakes were left?

_____ cupcakes

On Monday, we made 37 puff-ball chicks. On Tuesday, we made 20. On Wednesday, we made 29 more. On Thursday, Petey the Dog ate 12 puff-ball chicks. It was raining. How many puff-ball chicks did we have left?

_____ puff-ball chicks

Julio sorted his rock collection. He found the rocks at the beach last summer. He had 14 shiny rocks. He had 23 rough rocks. He had 17 smooth rocks. And he had 41 sparkly rocks. How many rocks did Julio have in his collection?

_____ rocks

Standard: Math | Operations & Algebraic Thinking | 2.OA.1   ©www.CoreCommonStandards.com

Level: Second Grade   Name: _____

More Adding and Subtracting Number Stories

Directions: Read the number stories below. Think about what information is important. Think about whether you should add or subtract. Draw pictures and equations to help you work out the problems.

Tula and her friend Rhonda were holding some flowers. They like flowers. Tula was holding 18 flowers. Together the girls had 35 flowers. How many flowers was Rhonda holding?

_____ flowers

Mom had 2 cookie jars on the counter. There were 48 cookies total in the jars. The first jar had 16 oatmeal cookies. How many cookies were in the other jar?

_____ cookies

Betsey and Kayla loved to play with Barbies. Betsey had 19 Barbies. Kayla had 15. For her birthday, Kayla received 5 more Barbies. How many Barbies do they have altogether now?

_____ Barbies

Jimmy had 98¢ in his pocket. He bought a bag of chips for 40¢, a licorice stick for 19¢, and a juice box for 20¢. How much money did Jimmy have left in his pocket after his snack?

_____ ¢

Standard: Math I Operations & Algebraic Thinking I 2.OA.1   ©www.CoreCommonStandards.com

Level: Second Grade   Name: _____

Adding To Twenty

Directions: Complete the addition equations below.

```
  15        16        20        11
+  4      +  3      +  0      +  3
____      ____      ____      ____
[  ]      [  ]      [  ]      [  ]

  13        10        11        12
+  4      +  9      +  9      +  6
____      ____      ____      ____
[  ]      [  ]      [  ]      [  ]
```

14 + 6 = [ ]   13 + 7 = [ ]

17 + 3 = [ ]   10 + 10 = [ ]

18 + 2 = [ ]   15 + 5 = [ ]

16 + 4 = [ ]   19 + 1 = [ ]

Level: Second Grade   Name: _____

Subtracting From Twenty

Directions: Complete the subtraction equations below.

```
  20        20        20        20
-  7      -  8      -  5      -  6
----      ----      ----      ----
[  ]      [  ]      [  ]      [  ]
```

```
  20        20        20        20
-  9      -  1      -  2      -  4
----      ----      ----      ----
[  ]      [  ]      [  ]      [  ]
```

20 - 13 = [   ]   20 - 11 = [   ]

20 - 16 = [   ]   20 - 19 = [   ]

20 - 17 = [   ]   20 - 14 = [   ]

20 - 18 = [   ]   20 - 12 = [   ]

Standard: Math l Operations & Algebraic Thinking l 2.OA.2   ©www.CoreCommonStandards.com

Level: Second Grade   Name: _____

Odd or Even

Directions: Look at the pictures below. By counting the pictures, or using counters, split the pictures into two equal groups. Write an equation with two equal addends for each group.

1. 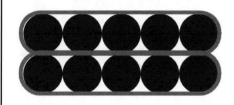 $5 + 5 = 10$	2.  ___ + ___ = ___	3.  ___ + ___ = ___
4.  ___ + ___ = ___	5. 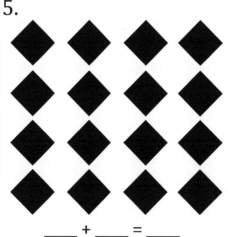 ___ + ___ = ___	6.  ___ + ___ = ___
7. 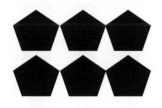 ___ + ___ = ___	8. 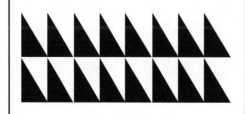 ___ + ___ = ___	9. 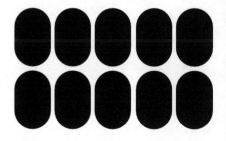 ___ + ___ = ___

Standard: Math | Operations & Algebraic Thinking | 2.OA.3   ©www.CoreCommonStandards.com

Level: Second Grade Name: _____

Odd or Even

Directions: Read the numbers below. Write <u>odd</u> or <u>even</u> under the correct numbers.

19	**3**	**10**	**12**
11	**8**	**20**	**9**
4	**17**	**14**	**5**
1	**18**	**15**	**7**
6	**2**	**16**	**13**

Choose four even numbers from above. Write an addition equation with two equal addends for each of the numbers you chose.

____ + ____ = ____   ____ + ____ = ____

____ + ____ = ____   ____ + ____ = ____

Standard: Math | Operations & Algebraic Thinking | 2.OA.3   ©www.CoreCommonStandards.com

Level: Second Grade   Name: _____

Adding and Arrays

Directions: Look at the arrays below. Write an addition equation for each array that tells the total number of squares. Try to write two equations for each array.

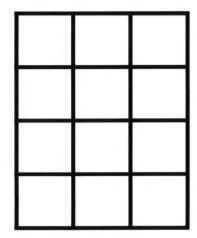

4 + 4 + 4 = 12
3 + 3 + 3 + 3 = 12

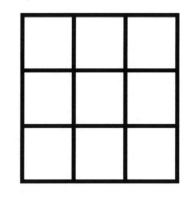

__ + __ + __ = __

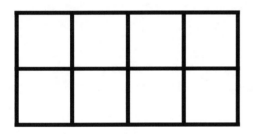

__ + __ + __ + __ = __

__ + __ = __

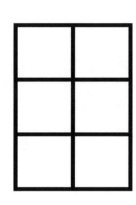

__ + __ = __

__ + __ + __ = __

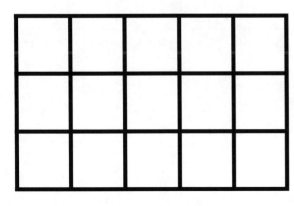

__ + __ + __ + __ + __ = __

__ + __ + __ = __

Standard: Math | Operations & Algebraic Thinking | 2.OA.4   ©www.CoreCommonStandards.com

Level: Second Grade   Name: _____

Addition and Arrays

Directions: Look at the arrays below. Write an addition equation for each array that tells the total number of squares. Try to write two equations for each array.

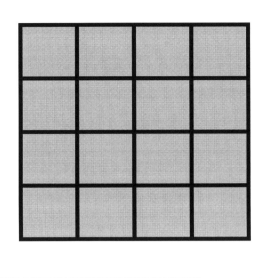

_____

_____

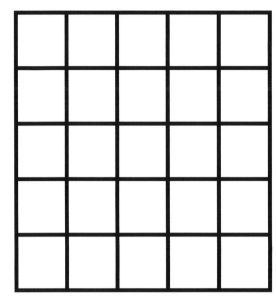

_____

_____

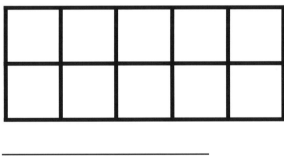

_____

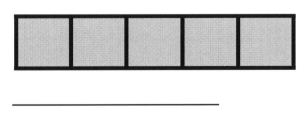

_____

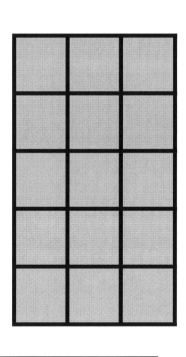

_____

_____

Standard: Math I Operations & Algebraic Thinking I 2.OA.4   ©www.CoreCommonStandards.com

Level: Second Grade   Name: _____

Hundreds, Tens, and Ones

Directions: Read the three-digit numbers below. Think about the place of each digit. Which digit is in the hundreds place, tens place, and ones place in each number?

271 ___hundreds ___tens ___ones	**418** ___hundreds ___tens ___ones
523 ___hundreds ___tens ___ones	**849** ___hundreds ___tens ___ones
740 ___hundreds ___tens ___ones	**642** ___hundreds ___tens ___ones
339 ___hundreds ___tens ___ones	**967** ___hundreds ___tens ___ones

Standard: Math | Number & Operations in Base Ten | 2.NBT.1   ©www.CoreCommonStandards.com

Level: Second Grade   Name: _____

Hundreds, Tens, and Ones

Directions: Read the three-digit numbers below. Think about the place of each digit. Which digit is in the hundreds place, tens place, and ones place in each number?

502 ___tens ___hundreds ___ones	673 ___ones ___tens ___hundreds
981 ___hundreds ___ones ___tens	720 ___hundreds ___tens ___ones
487 ___ones ___hundreds ___tens	199 ___hundreds ___ones ___tens
363 ___ones ___hundreds ___tens	804 ___tens ___ones ___hundreds

Standard: Math | Number & Operations in Base Ten | 2.NBT.1   ©www.CoreCommonStandards.com

I Can Count to One Thousand by Fives

Level: Second Grade Name: _____

Directions: Continue the counts below by fives.

55	60	65	70	75	80	85	90	95	100	105	110	115

235	240	245	250	255	260	265	270	275	280	285	290	295

730	735	740	745	750	755	760	765	770	775	780	785	790

305	310	315	320	325	330	335	340	345	350	355	360	365

610	615	620	625	630	635	640	645	650	655	660	665	670

860	865	870	875	880	885	890	895	900	905	910	915	920

440	445	450	455	460	465	470	475	480	485	490	495	500

155	160	165	170	175	180	185	190	195	200	205	210	215

785	790	795	800	805	810	815	820	825	830	835	840	845

495	500	505	510	515	520	525	530	535	540	545	550	555

935	940	945	950	955	960	965	970	975	980	985	990	995

Standard: Math | Numbers & Operations in Base Ten | 2.NBT.2 ©www.CoreCommonStandards.com

Level: Second Grade   Name: _____

I Can Count to One Thousand by Fives

Directions: Continue the counts below by fives.   Answer Key

55	60	65	70	75	80	85	90	95	100	105	110	115	120
235	240	245	250	255	260	265	270	275	280	285	290	295	300
730	735	740	745	750	755	760	765	770	775	780	785	790	795
305	310	315	320	325	330	335	340	345	350	355	360	365	370
610	615	620	625	630	635	640	645	650	655	660	665	670	675
855	860	865	870	875	880	885	890	895	900	905	910	915	920
440	445	450	455	460	465	470	475	480	485	490	495	500	505
155	160	165	170	175	180	185	190	195	200	205	210	215	220
785	790	795	800	805	810	815	820	825	830	835	840	845	850
495	500	505	510	515	520	525	530	535	540	545	550	555	560
935	940	945	950	955	960	965	970	975	980	985	990	995	1000

Standard: Math I Numbers & Operations in Base Ten I 2.NBT.2   ©www.CoreCommonStandards.com

Level: Second Grade   Name: _____

I Can Count to 1000 by Tens & Hundreds

Directions: Continue the counts below by tens.

70						130							

		240											

	580						650						

850					910								

	400					450							

720							800						

		330								410			

	610											720	

Directions: Continue the counts below by hundreds.

100										

*400										

Standard: Math I Numbers & Operations in Base Ten I 2.NBT.2   ©www.CoreCommonStandards.com

Level: Second Grade   Name: _____

I Can Count to One Thousand by Fives

Directions: Continue the counts below by tens.   Answer Key

| 70 | 80 | 90 | 100 | 110 | 120 | 130 | 140 | 150 | 160 | 170 | 180 | 190 | 200 |

| 220 | 230 | 240 | 250 | 260 | 270 | 280 | 290 | 300 | 310 | 320 | 330 | 340 | 350 |

| 570 | 580 | 590 | 600 | 610 | 620 | 630 | 640 | 650 | 660 | 670 | 680 | 690 | 700 |

| 850 | 860 | 870 | 880 | 890 | 900 | 910 | 920 | 930 | 940 | 950 | 960 | 970 | 980 |

| 390 | 400 | 410 | 420 | 430 | 440 | 450 | 460 | 470 | 480 | 490 | 500 | 510 | 520 |

| 720 | 730 | 740 | 750 | 760 | 770 | 780 | 790 | 800 | 810 | 820 | 830 | 840 | 850 |

| 310 | 320 | 330 | 340 | 350 | 360 | 370 | 380 | 390 | 400 | 410 | 420 | 430 | 440 |

| 600 | 610 | 620 | 630 | 640 | 650 | 660 | 670 | 680 | 690 | 700 | 710 | 720 | 730 |

Directions: Continue the counts below by hundreds.

| 100 | 200 | 300 | 400 | 500 | 600 | 700 | 800 | 900 | 1000 |

| 400 | 500 | 600 | 700 | 800 | 900 | 1000 | 1010 | 1020 | 1030 |

Standard: Math | Numbers & Operations in Base Ten | 2.NBT.2   ©www.CoreCommonStandards.com

Level: Second Grade   Name: _____

Writing Numbers

Directions: Read the three-digit numbers below.   Write the number names for each hundreds number written.

567   Five hundred sixty-seven
391   _____
472   _____
813   _____
906   _____
755   _____
684   _____
249   _____

Standard: Math I Number & Operations in Base Ten I 2.NBT.3   ©www.CoreCommonStandards.com

Level: Second Grade   Name: _____

Expanding Numbers

<u>Directions:</u> Read the three-digit numbers below.   Write the expanded form for each hundreds number.

468   400 + 60 + 8
592   _____
912   _____
763   _____
841   _____
608   _____
359   _____
218   _____

Standard: Math I Number & Operations in Base Ten I 2.NBT.3   ©www.CoreCommonStandards.com

Level: Second Grade   Name: _____

Comparing Hundreds, Tens and Ones

Directions: Compare the three-digit numbers. Think about tens and ones.
Write in <, =, or > to make the equation true.

<   =   >

517 __ 419	527 __ 538	331 __ 374
202 __ 203	665 __ 656	413 __ 473
885 __ 628	973 __ 937	441 __ 441
204 __ 502	163 __ 163	583 __ 930
521 __ 521	678 __ 634	130 __ 350
900 __ 900	516 __ 615	247 __ 427
668 __ 866	538 __ 835	702 __ 702

Standard: Math | Number & Operations in Base Ten | 2.NBT.4   ©www.CoreCommonStandards.com

Level: Second Grade   Name: _____

Comparing Hundreds, Tens and Ones

Directions: Compare the three-digit numbers. Think about hundreds, tens and ones. Write in <, =, or > to make the equation true. Then, write how you know it is true.

456 ___ 478 478 is greater than 456 because 7 tens is more than 5 tens. or 478 is greater than 456 because 78 has 22 more ones than 56.	**320 ___ 311**
539 ___ 521	**725 ___ 745**
803 ___ 308	**567 ___ 567**
936 ___ 900	**683 ___ 645**

Standard: Math | Number & Operations in Base Ten | 2.NBT.4   ©www.CoreCommonStandards.com

Level: Second Grade   Name: _____

Adding To One Hundred

Directions: Add the tens and ones below.   Use the strategies you have learned to help you.

```
  34        25        28        19
+ 66      + 47      + 58      + 38
```

```
  49        29        77        82
+ 36      + 47      + 15      + 10
```

43 + 27 =   55 + 37 =

28 + 30 =   29 + 49 =

17 + 33 =   62 + 18 =

35 + 44 =   70 + 27 =

Standard: Math I Number & Operations in Base Ten I 2.NBT.5   ©www.CoreCommonStandards.com

Level: Second Grade   Name: _____

0	1	2	3	4	5	6	7	8	9
10	11	12	13	14	15	16	17	18	19
20	21	22	23	24	25	26	27	28	29
30	31	32	33	34	35	36	37	38	39
40	41	42	43	44	45	46	47	48	49
50	51	52	53	54	55	56	57	58	59
60	61	62	63	64	65	66	67	68	69
70	71	72	73	74	75	76	77	78	79
80	81	82	83	84	85	86	87	88	89
90	91	92	93	94	95	96	97	98	99
100									

Standard: Math I Number & Operations in Base Ten I 2.NBT.5   ©www.CoreCommonStandards.com

Level: Second Grade   Name: _____

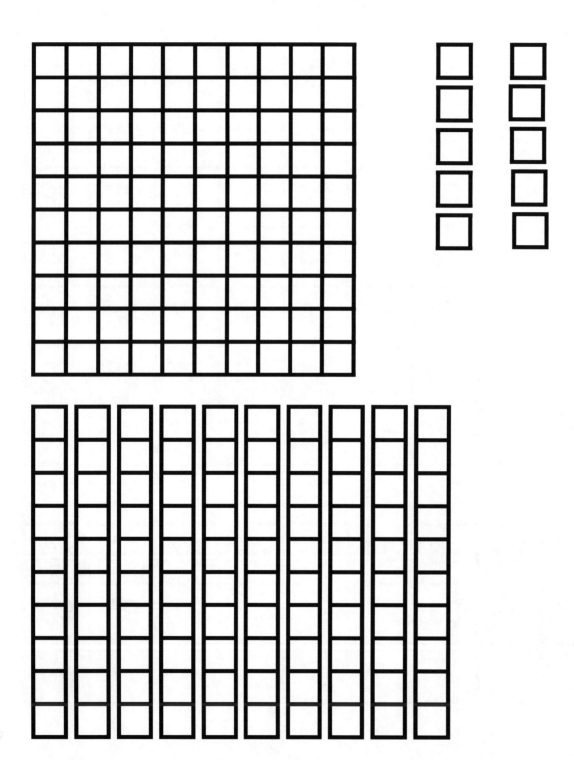

Standard: Math | Number & Operations in Base Ten | 2.NBT.5   ©www.CoreCommonStandards.com

Level: Second Grade   Name: _____

Subtracting From One Hundred

Directions: Subtract the tens and ones below. Use the strategies you have learned to help

```
  88         57         94         78
- 36       - 36       - 45       - 39
```

```
  48         94         89         77
- 23       - 57       - 38       - 24
```

77 - 38 = ☐   92 - 45 = ☐

100 - 25 = ☐   83 - 62 = ☐

100 - 34 = ☐   56 - 14 = ☐

86 - 50 = ☐   73 - 34 = ☐

Standard: Math | Number & Operations in Base Ten | 2.NBT.5   ©www.CoreCommonStandards.com

Level: Second Grade   Name: _____

0	1	2	3	4	5	6	7	8	9
10	11	12	13	14	15	16	17	18	19
20	21	22	23	24	25	26	27	28	29
30	31	32	33	34	35	36	37	38	39
40	41	42	43	44	45	46	47	48	49
50	51	52	53	54	55	56	57	58	59
60	61	62	63	64	65	66	67	68	69
70	71	72	73	74	75	76	77	78	79
80	81	82	83	84	85	86	87	88	89
90	91	92	93	94	95	96	97	98	99
100									

Standard: Math | Number & Operations in Base Ten | 2.NBT.5   ©www.CoreCommonStandards.com

Level: Second Grade   Name: _____

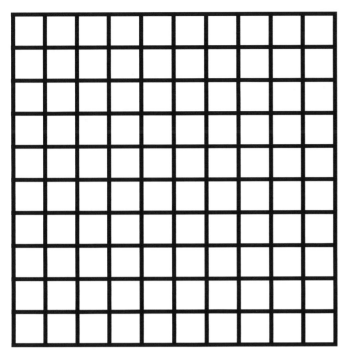
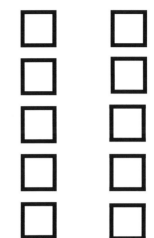
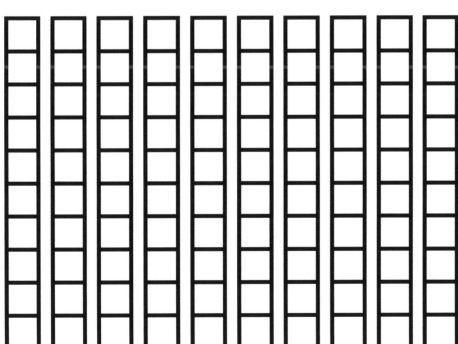

Standard: Math I Number & Operations in Base Ten I 2.NBT.5   ©www.CoreCommonStandards.com

Level: First Grade   Name: _____

Adding Two-Digit Numbers

Directions: Add the 2-digit numbers together. Look at the tens and ones to help you.

Here's a trick... add the tens, then add the ones. Then add the tens and ones together.

48 + 37 = *40 + 30* and *8 + 7* = **70 + 15 = 85**
35 + 12 + 44 = *30 + 10 + 40* and *5 + 2 + 4* = **80 + 11 = 91**

35 + 46 =	39 + 56 =
38 + 19 + 22 =	23 + 20 + 41
12 + 32 + 45 + 10 =	22 + 31 + 42 + 38 =

Standard: Math l Number & Operations in Base Ten l 2.NBT.6   ©www.CoreCommonStandards.com

Level: Second Grade   Name: _____

Adding Two-Digit Numbers

Directions: Look at the data sheet below. Use the information to solve the addition equations.

Number of Colored Marbles in Maxwell's Treasure Chest

red	45	orange	53
blue	67	pink	94
green	32	violet	70
yellow	81	indigo	28

What is the total number of red, orange, yellow, and blue marbles?

red _____

orange _____

yellow _____

blue _____

What is the total number of indigo, pink, orange, and blue marbles?

indigo _____

pink _____

orange _____

blue _____

What is the total number of violet, red, green, and yellow marbles?

violet _____

red _____

green _____

yellow _____

What is the total number of green, indigo, red, and pink marbles?

green _____

indigo _____

red _____

pink _____

Standard: Math | Number & Operations in Base Ten | 2.NBT.6   ©www.CoreCommonStandards.com

Level: Second Grade   Name: _____

Adding Within One Thousand

Directions: Add the 3-digit numbers together. Look at the tens, ones, and hundreds to help you.

You may use objects, such as base-ten blocks, or drawings to help.

Th	H	T	O
	5	2	1
+	3	1	8

Th	H	T	O
	2	7	3
+	5	0	6

Th	H	T	O
	8	0	2
+	1	7	3

Th	H	T	O
	8	1	5
+	1	7	0

Th	H	T	O
	4	6	3
+	3	3	7

Th	H	T	O
	2	8	6
+	5	6	9

Th	H	T	O
	3	2	1
+	3	1	8

Th	H	T	O
	5	2	1
+	3	1	8

Th	H	T	O
	7	4	7
+	1	0	8

Standard: Math | Number & Operations in Base Ten | 2.NBT.7   ©www.CoreCommonStandards.com

Level: Second Grade   Name: _____

Subtracting Within One Thousand

Directions: Subtract the numbers below. Look at the tens, ones, and hundreds to help you.

You may use objects, such as base-ten blocks, or drawings to help.

Th H T O	Th H T O	Th H T O
9 3 7 − 6 2 5	9 6 2 − 8 5 1	9 8 3 − 7 4 0
9 9 9 − 5 6 8	8 7 4 − 7 5 2	8 9 5 − 7 5 3
* 9 4 3 − 7 5 2	* 9 0 2 − 6 1 5	* 1 0 0 0 − 7 3 4

Standard: Math | Number & Operations in Base Ten | 2.NBT.7   ©www.CoreCommonStandards.com

Level: Second Grade   Name: _____

Adding and Subtracting 10 and 100

Directions: Mentally add and subtract the numbers below. Think about tens and hundreds.

Add 10 to 200 : 200...210   Subtract 100 from 640 : 640...540
          (+10)   (-100)

Add 10 to 300 : _____	Add 10 to 570 : _____
Add 100 to 700 : _____	Add 10 to 820 : _____
Add 10 to 135 : _____	Add 100 to 286 : _____
Add 100 to 603 : _____	Add 10 to 492 : _____
Subtract 10 from 100 : _____	Subtract 100 from 900 : _____
Subtract 100 from 470 : _____	Subtract 10 from 860 : _____
Subtract 10 from 899 : _____	Subtract 100 from 552 : _____
Subtract 100 from 721 : _____	Subtract 10 from 385 : _____

Standard: Math l Number & Operations in Base Ten l 2.NBT.8   ©www.CoreCommonStandards.com

Level: Second Grade   Name: _____

Adding and Subtracting 10 and 100

Directions: Mentally add and subtract to solve the number stories below. Think about tens and hundreds.

        Add 10 to 200 : 200...210   Subtract 100 from 640 : 640...540
                    (+10)   (-100)

Paulo counted is marbles. He had 347 marbles. His sister, Jacklyn, came by and took 10 marbles. How many marbles does Paulo have now?

_____ marbles

There were 467 stickers on Annabelle's chart. Last month, she received 100 more stickers. How many stickers does Annabelle have now?

_____ stickers

Louis had 783 dollars in his bank account. Yesterday he bought an mp3 player that cost 100 dollars. How much money does Louis have in his bank account now?

_____ dollars

Chef Antoine cooked 546 stuffed mushrooms for the guests. He was asked to make 10 more for the band. How many total stuffed mushrooms did Chef Antoine cook?

_____ stuffed mushrooms

***Jillian and Phoebe collected 746 acorns last week. This week they had only 646 acorns. They think squirrels ate the rest. How many acorns did the squirrels at?

_____ acorns

Standard: Math I Number & Operations in Base Ten I 2.NBT.8   ©www.CoreCommonStandards.com

Level: Second Grade   Name: _____

Why it Works: Explaining Addition and Subtraction

Directions: Solve the following problems. Write, draw, or use equations and diagrams to explain what strategies you used to solve the problems. (Or, explain your thinking to your teacher.)

How does 4 + 5 help you solve 5 + 4?

Solve:

5 + 3 + 7 = _____

What strategy did you use to solve this equation?

Solve Mentally

37 + 24 = _____

What strategy did you use to solve this equation?

Solve Mentally

64 - 28 = _____

What strategy did you use to solve this equation?

Use the open number line to show the difference.

73 - 40 = _____

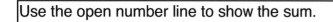

Use the open number line to show the sum.

56 + 37 = _____

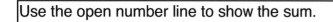

Standard: Math | Number & Operations in Base Ten | 2.NBT.9   ©www.CoreCommonStandards.com

Level: Second Grade   Name: _____

Why it Works: Explaining Addition and Subtraction

Directions: Solve the following problems. Write, draw, or use equations and diagrams to explain what strategies you used to solve the problems. (Or, explain your thinking to your teacher.)

Show why this equation is true.   13 + 6 = 10 + 9

Solve: What strategy did you use to solve this equation?

4 + 4 + 4 + 4 =

Solve Mentally   What strategy did you use to solve this equation?

135 + 10 = _____

Solve Mentally   What strategy did you use to solve this equation?

560 - 100 = _____

Use the open number line to show the difference.

85 - 67 = _____

⬅───────────────────────➡

Use the open number line to show the sum.

47 + 38 = _____

⬅───────────────────────➡

Standard: Math | Number & Operations in Base Ten | 2.NBT.9   ©www.CoreCommonStandards.com

Level: Second Grade   Name: _____

Measuring with Tools

Directions: Look around your classroom to find objects to measure. Decide which tool would best work for each object. Some measuring tools you may use are rulers, yardsticks, meter sticks, and measuring tapes. Write the name of the object and its length. You can also draw a picture. Use the proper unit in your response. [in, ft, yd, cm, m]

I measured _____ The length of my object is _____.	I measured _____ The length of my object is _____.
I measured _____ The length of my object is _____.	I measured _____ The length of my object is _____.
I measured _____ The length of my object is _____.	I measured _____ The length of my object is _____.

Standard: Math | Measurement & Data | 2.MD.1   ©www.CoreCommonStandards.com

Level: Second Grade   Name: _____

Measuring with Tools

Directions: Circle the tool that would be the best choice to use to measure the following objects.

a pencil	ruler	yardstick	measuring tape
jumprope	ruler	yardstick	measuring tape
school bus	ruler	yardstick	measuring tape
head	ruler	yardstick	measuring tape
paperclip	ruler	yardstick	measuring tape
picnic table	ruler	yardstick	measuring tape
rug	ruler	yardstick	measuring tape
globe	ruler	yardstick	measuring tape
child	ruler	yardstick	measuring tape

Standard: Math | Measurement & Data | 2.MD.1   ©www.CoreCommonStandards.com

Level: Second Grade   Name: _____

Measuring Objects

<u>Directions:</u> Measure the objects below to the nearest whole unit using two different units, such as centimeters and inches. Write the total number of units for each object.

The fishing rod is _____ _____ long and _____ _____ long.
　　　　　　　　(length)　　(units)　　　　　　　(length)　　(units)

....

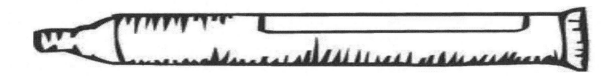

The crayon is _____ _____ long and _____ _____ long.
　　　　　　(length)　　(units)　　　　　　　(length)　　(units)

....

The spoon is _____ _____ long and _____ _____ long.
　　　　　　(length)　　(units)　　　　　　　(length)　　(units)

....

The pen is _____ _____ long and _____ _____ long.
　　　　　(length)　　(units)　　　　　　　(length)　　(units)

....

Standard: Math | Measurement & Data | 2.MD.2   ©www.CoreCommonStandards.com

Level: Second Grade   Name: _____

Measuring Objects

Directions: Measure the objects below to the nearest whole unit using two different units, such as centimeters and inches. Write the total number of units for each object. Are the measurements for each object the same?

The boat is _____ _____ long and _____ _____ long.
            (length)   (units)   (length)   (units)

What do you notice about the measurements?_____

. . . .

The lizard is _____ _____ long and _____ _____ long.
            (length)   (units)   (length)   (units)

What do you notice about the measurements?_____

. . . .

The truck is _____ _____ long and _____ _____ long.
            (length)   (units)   (length)   (units)

What do you notice about the measurements?_____

. . . .

The telescope is _____ _____ long and _____ _____ long.
                 (length)   (units)   (length)   (units)

What do you notice about the measurements?_____

. . . .

Standard: Math | Measurement & Data | 2.MD.2   ©www.CoreCommonStandards.com

Level: Second Grade   Name: _____

Estimating Measurements

Directions: Complete the web below with objects that could be measured with the unit named in the center.

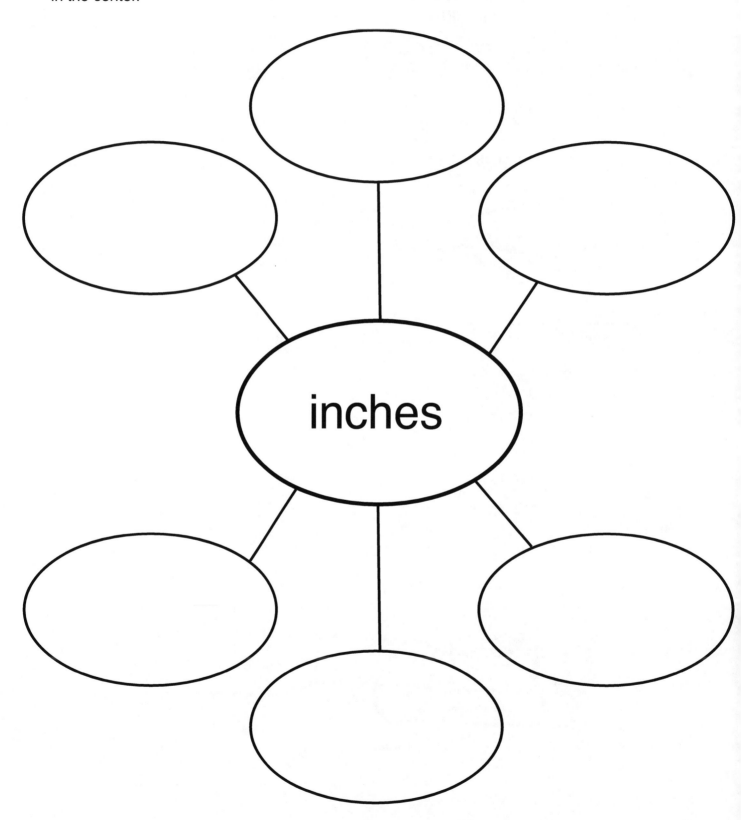

Standard: Math | Measurement & Data | 2.MD.3   ©www.CoreCommonStandards.com

124

Level: Second Grade Name: _____

Estimating Measurements

Directions: Complete the web below with objects that could be measured with the unit named in the center.

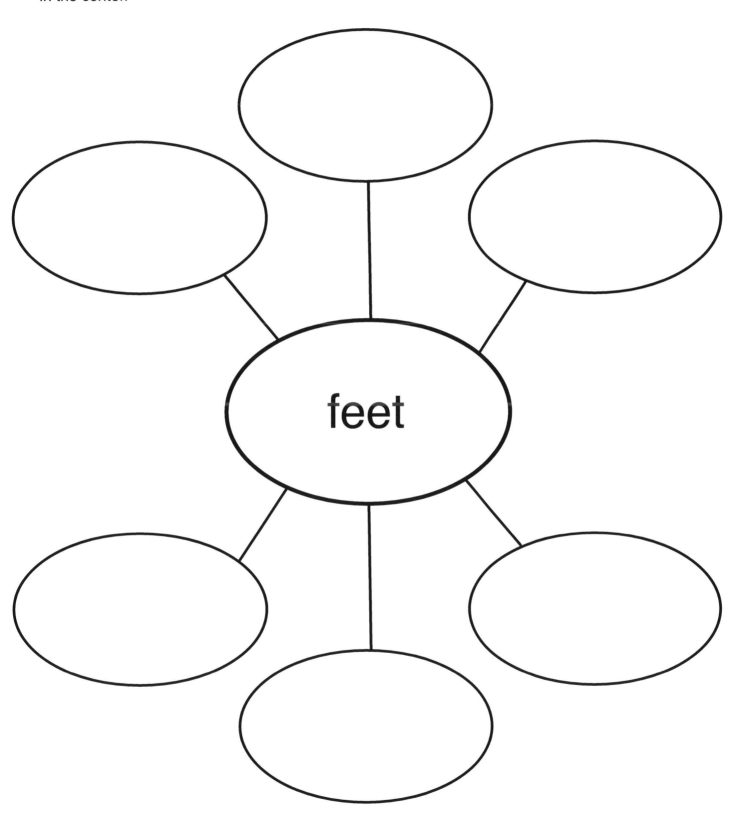

Standard: Math | Measurement & Data | 2.MD.3 ©www.CoreCommonStandards.com

Level: Second Grade   Name: _____

Estimating Measurements

Directions: Complete the web below with objects that could be measured with the unit named in the center.

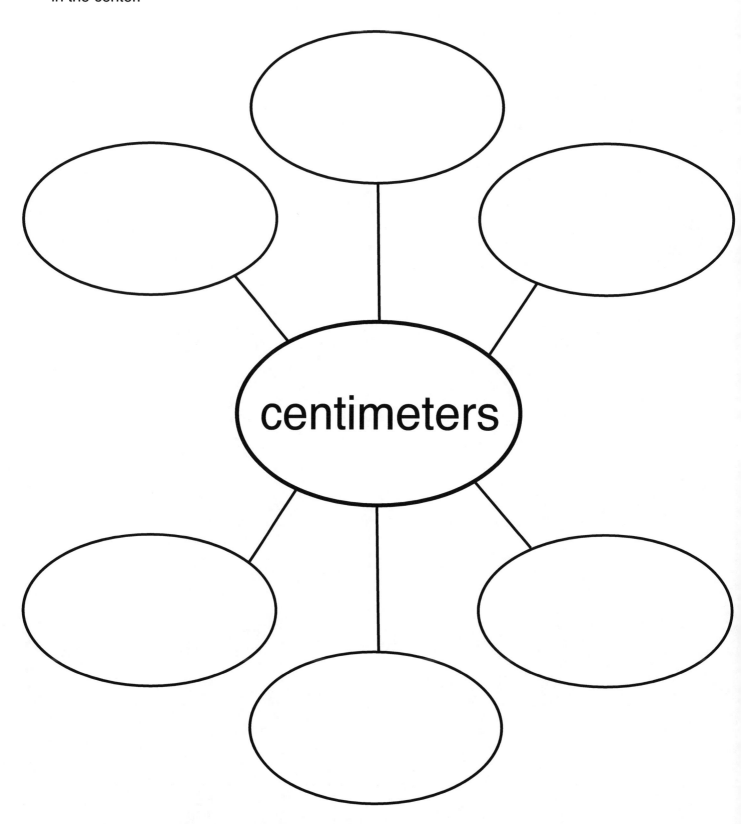

Standard: Math | Measurement & Data | 2.MD.3   ©www.CoreCommonStandards.com

Level: Second Grade   Name: _____

Estimating Measurements

Directions: Complete the web below with objects that could be measured with the unit named in the center.

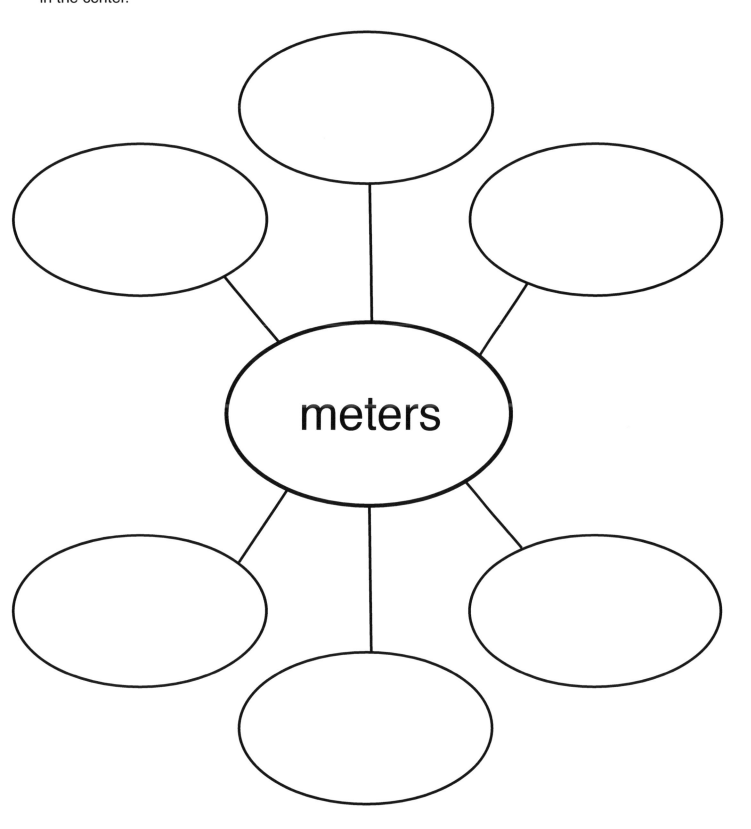

Standard: Math I Measurement & Data I 2.MD.3   ©www.CoreCommonStandards.com

Level: Second Grade   Name: _____

Estimating and Measuring with Tools

Directions: Estimate what unit, *inches, feet, centimeters, or meters*, would best work to measure the objects below. Write your estimate. Then measure. Did you choose the correct unit? Measure the object and record it's length below.

Object	Unit Estimate	Correct or Incorrect Choice?	Actual Measurement
paper clip			
window			
floor tile			
pencil			
classroom wall			
glue stick			
chalkboard			
door			

Standard: Math | Measurement & Data | 2.MD.3   ©www.CoreCommonStandards.com

Level: Second Grade   Name: _____

Measuring Objects

<u>Directions:</u> Measure each of the objects below in centimeters. Round to the nearest whole number.

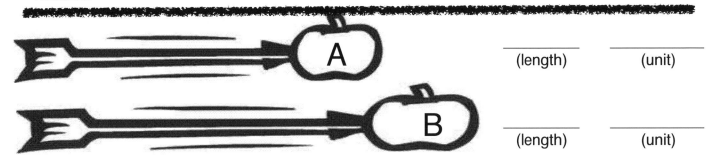

_____ _____
(length) (unit)

_____ _____
(length) (unit)

Arrow B is _____ _____ longer then Arrow A.
            (length)   (unit)

_____ _____
(length) (unit)

_____ _____
(length) (unit)

Fish C is _____ _____ longer then Fish D.
       (length)   (unit)

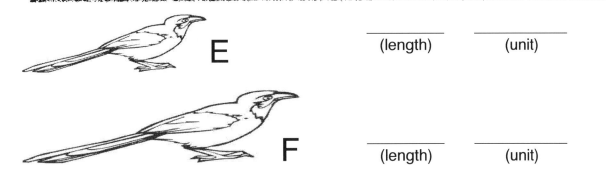

_____ _____
(length) (unit)

_____ _____
(length) (unit)

Bird F is _____ _____ longer then Bird E.
       (length)   (unit)

Standard: Math I Measurement & Data I 2.MD.4   ©www.CoreCommonStandards.com

Level: Second Grade   Name: _____

Adding with Measures

Directions: Solve the addition problems. You may use drawings and equations to show your work.

Candace's class made a paper chain that was 25 feet long. Kyle's class made a chain that was 37 feet long. They combined the two chains to make one. How long was the new chain?

_____ feet

____ + ____ = ____

Last week, dad built 8 meters of fence. This week he built 13 meters of fence. How much fence has he built so far?

_____ meters

____ + ____ = ____

I measured my kitchen table and it was 48 inches long. I measured the counter and it was 36 inches long. How many inches total did I measure?

_____ inches

____ + ____ = ____

Last month we had 44 centimeters of snowfall. This month we had 30. How much snowfall have we had so far?

_____ centimeters

____ + ____ = ____

***The school bus is 5 meters long. 3 buses are lined up front to back. How many meters long is the line of buses?

_____ meters

____ + ____ + ____ = ____

Standard: Math | Measurement & Data | 2.MD.5   ©www.HaveFunTeaching.com

Level: Second Grade   Name: _____

Subtracting with Measures

Directions: Solve the subtraction problems. You may use drawings and equations to show your work.

Peter has a snake that is 8 feet long. Bryan has a snake that is 10 feet long. How much longer is Bryan's snake than Peter's?

_____ feet

_____ - _____ = _____

The cell phone tower is 20 meters high. The fire watch tower is 3 meters shorter than the cell phone tower. How tall is the fire watch tower?

_____ meters

_____ - _____ = _____

Jake made a paperclip chain that was 57 inches long. Sean's paperclip chain was 76 inches long. How much longer was Sean's paperclip chain?

_____ inches

_____ - _____ = _____

John had a licorice stick that was 45 centimeters long. He ate 16 centimeters after lunch. How long is John's licorice stick now?

_____ centimeters

_____ - _____ = _____

In 2010, it rained 61 inches. In 2011, it rained 55 inches. How much less did it rain in 2011 than in 2010?

_____ inches

_____ - _____ = _____

Standard: Math | Measurement & Data | 2.MD.5   ©www.CoreCommonStandards.com

Level: Second Grade   Name: _____

Knowing your Number Line

Directions: Look at the number line. What numbers do the pictures represent?

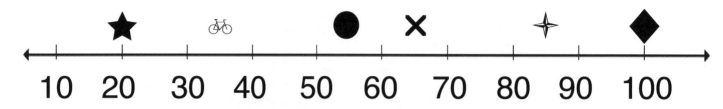

picture	number
🚲	
★	
✗	

picture	number
✦	
●	
◆	

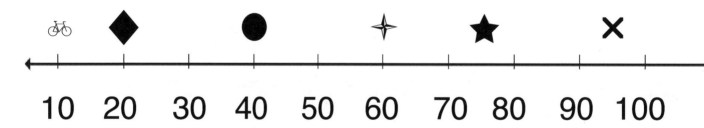

picture	number
🚲	
★	
✗	

picture	number
✦	
●	
◆	

Standard: Math | Measurement & Data | 2.MD.6   ©www.CoreCommonStandards.com

Level: Second Grade   Name: _____

Adding and Subtraction on a Number Line

Directions: Use the number lines to add and subtract the numbers represented by the pictures.

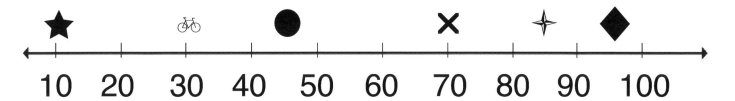

● - 🚲 = ☐   ✗ - ● = ☐

◆ - ★ = ☐   ✦ - 🚲 = ☐

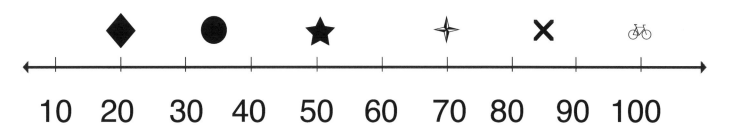

◆ + ✗ = ☐   ✦ + ★ = ☐

● + 🚲 = ☐   🚲 + ✗ = ☐

Standard: Math | Measurement & Data | 2.MD.6   ©www.CoreCommonStandards.com

Level: Second Grade   Name: _____

What Time is It?

Directions: Look at the clocks below. What time is it? Write the digital times beneath the clocks.

_ _ : _ _   _ _ : _ _   _ _ : _ _

_ _ : _ _   _ _ : _ _   _ _ : _ _

_ _ : _ _   _ _ : _ _   _ _ : _ _

_ _ : _ _   _ _ : _ _   _ _ : _ _

Standard: Math | Measurement & Data | 2.MD.7   ©www.CoreCommonStandards.com

Level: Second Grade   Name: _____

What Time is It?

Directions: Look at the clocks below. Draw the hands correctly to show the digital time below each clock.   Hour ⟶   Minute ⟶

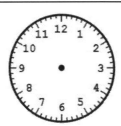 **4: 45**	**7: 15**	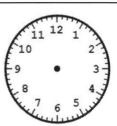 **2: 05**
 **9 : 35**	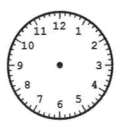 **6: 15**	 **10:20**
 **12:50**	 **1:55**	 **3:40**
 **5:30**	 **8: 10**	 **11:25**

Standard: Math l Measurement & Data l 2.MD.7   ©www.CoreCommonStandards.com

Level: Second Grade   Name: _____

Counting Money

Directions: Solve the money number stories below. Use the space to work out the problem. You can draw coins or write an equation. Use the $ or ¢ signs.

Julie opened her piggy bank and counted her coins. She had 4 pennies, 3 nickels, and 6 dimes. How much money did Julie have?

Barbara emptied all of her pockets and counted her money. She had 3 quarters, one dollar bill, and 14 pennies. How much money does Barbara have?

Kyle wrote down the money he received when sold lemonade. He had $3.00 in bills, $1.25 in quarters, 90¢ in dimes, and .30 in nickels. How much money did Kyle make?

Brendan has coins in his lunch box. He has 6 quarters, 5 dimes, 11 nickels, and 20 pennies. How much money does Brendan have?

***Lucy and Patty gathered their money together to see if they had enough to by a DVD. Lucy had 4 dollar bills, 3 quarters, and 6 dimes. Patty had $5.00 in quarters and .80 in dimes. How much money did they have?

Standard: Math | Measurement & Data | 2.MD.8   ©www.CoreCommonStandards.com

Level: Second Grade   Name: _____

Counting Money

Directions: Solve the money number stories below. Use the space to work out the problem. You can draw coins or write an equation. Use the $ or ¢ signs.

Karen had $3.10. Mary had $4.50. How much more money did Mary have than Karen?

Shandra bought a toy for 50¢. She paid the cashier with $1.00. How much change did Shandra get back?

Kayleigh had 35¢ in her purse. Susan had 73¢ in her pocket. How much money did they have together?

Paulie bought an ice cream for .25, a drink for .80, and a cookie for .35. How much money did Paulie spend?

Chloe had forty-five cents in a box and thirty-seven cents in a bag. She found a quarter on the ground. How much money does Chloe have now?

Standard: Math | Measurement & Data | 2.MD.8   ©www.CoreCommonStandards.com

Level: Second Grade   Name: _____

Organizing Data

Directions: Organize the measurements listed below into a line plot. Use an X to mark the data.

object	length
spoon	6 inches
straw	9 inches
pencil	5 inches
remote control	9 inches
crayon	3 inches
toothpick	2 inches
popsicle stick	5 inches
candy cane	9 inches
marker	6 inches

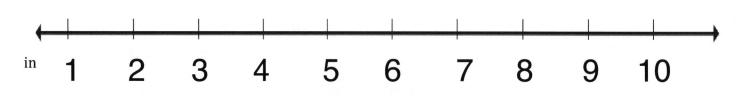

Standard: Math | Measurement & Data | 2.MD.9   ©www.CoreCommonStandards.com

Level: Second Grade   Name: _____

Organizing Data

Directions: Organize the measurements listed below into a line plot. Use an X to mark the data.

object	length
book	6 inches
calculator	3 inches
crayon	2 inches
crayon box	4 inches
glue bottle	4 inches
lunch box	6 inches
paper	10 inches
pencil	4 inches
scissors	4 inches
desk	10 inches
chalk	3 inches

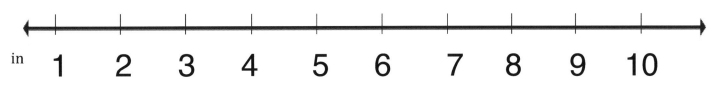

Standard: Math | Measurement & Data | 2.MD.9   ©www.CoreCommonStandards.com

Level: Second Grade   Name: _____

Organizing Data

Directions: Organize the measurements listed below into a line plot. Use an X to mark the data.

object	length
microphone	6 inches
robot	8 inches
teddy bear	12 inches
doll	8 inches
video game	2 inches
train	4 inches
car	4 inches
ball	5 inches
pillow	14 inches
book	8 inches

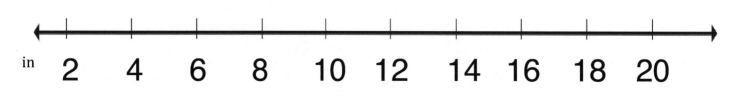

Standard: Math | Measurement & Data | 2.MD.9   ©www.CoreCommonStandards.com

Level: Second Grade   Name: _____

Organizing Data

Directions: Organize the measurements listed below into a line plot. Use an X to mark the data.

object	length
computer screen	3 feet
model train	5 feet
picture frame	7 feet
door	9 feet
table	4 feet
sink	3 feet
oven	5 feet
cabinet	3 feet
counter top	8 feet
refrigerator	7 feet

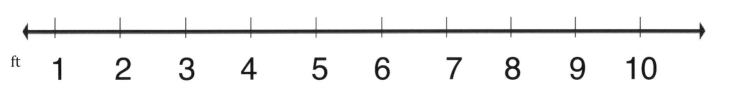

Standard: Math | Measurement & Data | 2.MD.9   ©www.CoreCommonStandards.com

Level: Second Grade   Name: _____

Graphing Animals at the Shelter

Directions: Look at the data below. Arrange the data and organize it into a graph.

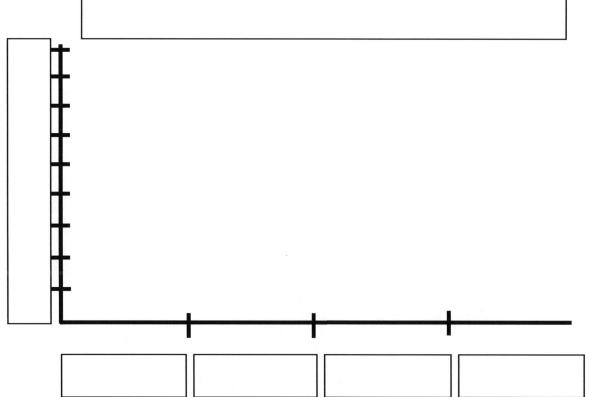

Standard: Math | Measurement & Data | 2.MD.10   ©www.CoreCommonStandards.com

Name: _____

Graphing Animals at the Shelter

Directions: Using the data and the graph you made, answer the questions below.

1. How many dogs are at the shelter?

   _____

2. How many pigs are at the shelter?

   _____

3. How many more dogs are there than birds at the animal shelter?

   _____

4. How many animals are there altogether?

   _____

5. What is the total amount of birds and pigs at the shelter?

   _____

Standard: Math | Measurement & Data | 2.MD.10   ©www.CoreCommonStandards.com

Level: Second Grade   Name: _____

Graphing Favorite Foods

Directions: Look at the data below. Arrange the data and organize it into a graph.

Name	Favorite Food	Name	Favorite Food
Lucy	pizza	Tracey	spaghetti
Andy	spaghetti	Harold	spaghetti
Kyle	tacos	Donna	pizza
Sharon	spaghetti	Wayne	hamburger
Phil	pizza	Linda	pizza
Manny	pizza	Nina	pizza
Abigail	tacos	Bruce	tacos
Claud	hamburger	Ophelia	hamburger
Simon	hamburger	Ashley	pizza

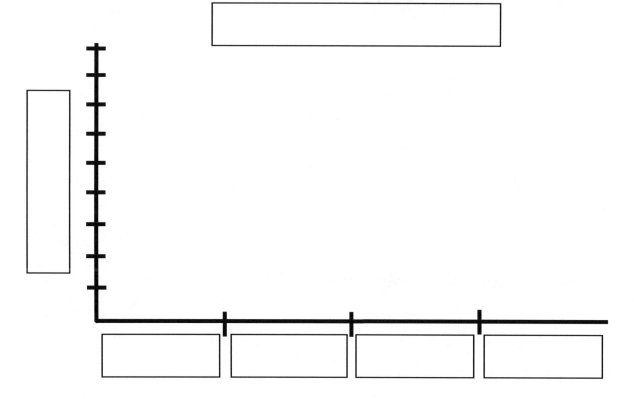

Standard: Math | Measurement & Data | 2.MD.10

Name: _____

Graphing Favorite Foods

Directions: Using the data and the graph you made, answer the questions below.

Name	Favorite Food	Name	Favorite Food
Lucy	pizza	Tracey	spaghetti
Andy	spaghetti	Harold	spaghetti
Kyle	tacos	Donna	pizza
Sharon	spaghetti	Wayne	hamburger
Phil	pizza	Linda	pizza
Manny	pizza	Nina	pizza
Abigail	tacos	Bruce	tacos
Claud	hamburger	Ophelia	hamburger
Simon	hamburger	Ashley	pizza

1. How many kids like pizza?

   _____

2. How many kids like spaghetti?

   _____

3. How many more kids like pizza than tacos?

   _____

4. How many kids total like tacos and hamburgers?

   _____

5. What is the total amount of kids that were surveyed?

   _____

Standard: Math | Measurement & Data | 2.MD.10   ©www.CoreCommonStandards.com

Level: Second Grade   Name: _____

Drawing Shapes with Rules

Directions: Draw shapes below that match the attributes written in the boxes.

Draw a shape with four angles.	Draw a shape with no straight sides.
Draw a 3D shape made of only squares.	Draw a 3D shape that has two circles.
Draw a shape that has more than four sides.	Draw a shape that rolls.

Standard: Math | Geometry | 2.G.1   ©www.CoreCommonStandards.com

Level: Second Grade   Name: _____

How Many Faces and Vertices?

Directions: Count and write the number of faces and vertices for each 3-dimensional shape.

faces: _____ vertices: _____	faces: _____ vertices: _____	faces: _____ vertices: _____
faces: _____ vertices: _____	faces: _____ vertices: _____	faces: _____ vertices: _____

Standard: Math l Geometry l 2.G.1   ©www.CoreCommonStandards.com

Level: Second Grade   Name: _____

What's Inside?

Directions: Count the number of same-size squares in each shape to find the area inside.

area inside:_____

area inside:_____

area inside:_____

area inside:_____

area inside:_____

area inside:_____

Standard: Math | Geometry | 2.G.2   ©www.CoreCommonStandards.com

Level: Second Grade   Name: _____

What's Inside?

Directions: Count the number of same-size squares in each shape to find the area inside.

area inside:_____

area inside:_____

area inside:_____

area inside:_____

area inside:_____

area inside:_____

Standard: Math | Geometry | 2.G.2   ©www.CoreCommonStandards.com

Level: Second Grade   Name: _____

Halves, Thirds, and Fourths

Directions: Shade in the proper amount. Write how much is shaded.

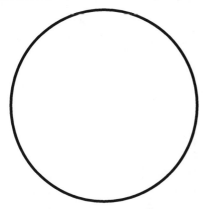

Partition this circle into two equal shares. Label the equal shares.

Partition this rectangle into four equal shares. Label the equal shares.

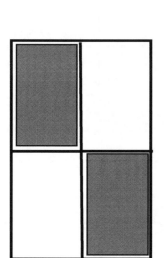

How much is shaded?

_____

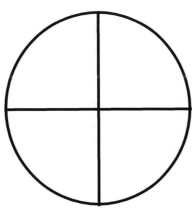

How much is shaded?

_____

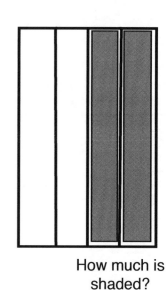

How much is shaded?

_____

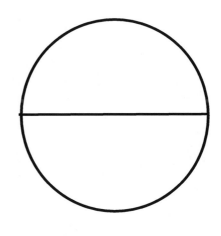

Shade three fourths.   Shade one half.

Standard: Math | Geometry | 2.G.3   ©www.CoreCommonStandards.com

150

Level: Second Grade					Name: _____

Halves, Thirds, and Fourths

Directions: Shade in the proper amount for each circle. Divide the rectangles to create equal parts, then shade.

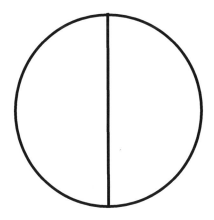 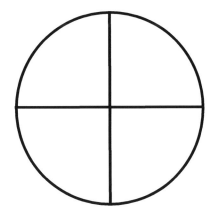 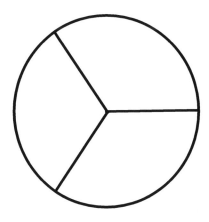

Shade one-half of the circle.   Shade two-fourths of the circle.   Shade one-third of the circle.

Divide the rectangle into four equal parts. Shade three-fourths.   Divide the rectangle into three equal parts. Shade two-thirds.   Divide the rectangle into four equal parts. Shade two-fourths.

Standard: Math | Geometry | 2.G.3					©www.CoreCommonStandards.com

Common Core State Standards
Educating classrooms one standard at a time.

Terms of Use

All worksheets, activities, workbooks and other printable materials purchased or downloaded from this website are protected under copyright law. Items purchased from this website may be used, copied and printed for classroom, personal and home use depending on how many licenses are purchased. Upon printing and copying the materials from this website, you must leave the Copyright Information at the bottom of each item printed. Items may not be copied or distributed unless you have purchased them from this website. Furthermore, you may not reproduce, sell, or copy these resources, or post on your website any Worksheet, Activity, PDF, Workbook, or Printable without written permission from Have Fun Teaching, LLC using the contact form below. All Common Core State Standards are from CoreStandards.org and the Common Core State Standards Initiative.

All Common Core State Standards in this book are © Copyright 2010. National Governors Association Center for Best Practices and Council of Chief State School Officers. All rights reserved. Furthermore, NGA Center/CCSSO are the sole owners and developers of the Common Core State Standards, and Core Common Standards makes no claims to the contrary.

All Graphics, Images, and Logos are © Copyright 2012 CoreCommonStandards.com. Also, the organization of this book and Table of Contents has been created by and organized by CoreCommonStandards.com and HaveFunTeaching.com.

Fore more Common Core Standards Posters, Activities, Worksheets, and Workbooks, visit http://CoreCommonStandards.com.

Worksheets created by: Have Fun Teaching
Activities created by: Have Fun Teaching
Posters created by: Have Fun Teaching

Made in the USA
Middletown, DE
08 November 2023

42143141R00086